SCOTTISH QUOTATIONS

BOOKS BY ALAN BOLD

POETRY

Society Inebrious
The Voyage
To Find The New
A Perpetual Motion Machine
Penguin Modern Poets 15 (with Brathwaite and Morgan)
The State Of The Nation
The Auld Symie
He Will Be Greatly Missed
A Century Of People
A Pint Of Bitter
Scotland, Yes
This Fine Day
A Celtic Quintet (with Bellany)
In This Corner: Selected Poems 1963-83
Haven (with Bellany)
Summoned By Knox

STORIES

Hammer And Thistle (with Morrison)
The Edge Of The Wood

NONFICTION

Thom Gunn And Ted Hughes
George Mackay Brown
The Ballad
The Sensual Scot
Modern Scottish Literature
MacDiarmid: The Terrible Crystal
True Characters (with Giddings)
The Book Of Rotters (with Giddings)

AS EDITOR

The Penguin Book Of Socialist Verse
The Martial Muse: Seven Centuries Of War Poetry
Cambridge Book Of English Verse 1939-75
Making Love: The Picador Book Of Erotic Verse
The Bawdy Beautiful: The Sphere Book Of Improper Verse
Mounts Of Venus: The Picador Book Of Erotic Prose
Drink To Me Only: The Prose (And Cons) Of Drinking
Smollett: Author Of The First Dimension
The Sexual Dimension In Literature
A Scottish Poetry Book
Scott: The Long-Forgotten Melody
Byron: Wrath And Rhyme
The Thistle Rises: A MacDiarmid Miscellany
MacDiarmid: Aesthetics In Scotland
The Letters Of Hugh MacDiarmid
The Poetry Of Motion
Muriel Spark: An Odd Capacity For Vision
Harold Pinter: You Never Heard Such Silence
Auden: The Far Interior

SCOTTISH
QUOTATIONS

Alan Bold

THE MERCAT PRESS

1985

EDINBURGH

JAMES THIN
The Mercat Press
53-59 South Bridge
Edinburgh

First published 1985

© Alan Bold

Design, typography, jacket and layouts by
T. L. Jenkins, Edinburgh.

Cover drawings of Robert Burns
and Hugh MacDiarmid by Alice Bold.

ISBN 0 901824 79 8

Printed in Scotland by Clark Constable (1982) Ltd.

CONTENTS

FOREWORD

Defending his decision to film MGM's tartan musical *Brigadoon* (1954) in Hollywood, producer Arthur Freed said 'I went to Scotland and found nothing there that looks like Scotland'. The various eloquent voices on the following pages tell a more convincing tale than that.

Though ostensibly a small nation of five million odd souls, Scotland is a large subject. Its natural drama has attracted the attention of great nonScots (such as Shakespeare, to cite one obvious example) while the native talent for self-expression has produced internationally appreciated authors as quotable as Burns, Hume, Adam Smith, Scott, Stevenson, and MacDiarmid to name a few.

This book gathers together some of the most memorable things that have been said by Scots and about Scotland. To contain, in one volume, the complexity of Scotland I have subdivided the text into twelve thematic sections. In each of these the quotations are arranged alphabetically by author; the exception to this rule is the section on 'Places' where the entries are arranged (predictably enough) alphabetically by place.

In the interests of the general reader I have provided headings for each entry. For the purposes of reference there is also a Subject Index of First Lines and an Index of Authors. Sources of quotations are given in some detail, whenever possible by noting place of publication, publisher and page numbers for particular titles, though this approach does not always apply to classics available in a number of editions.

I am most grateful to all the modern writers represented for allowing me to quote copyright material.

ALAN BOLD

1

AS OTHERS SEE US

AFTER A DRAM

O Caledonia
Fair and wild
Bitter as bitter
Mild as mild
But the blood of a Scot
When he's had a dram
Couldn't be stopped
By Boulder Dam ...

GEORGE BARKER, (born 1913),
'Scottish Bards and an English Reviewer'

A DOUBLE DOSE

For Scotland has a double dose of the poison called heredity;
the sense of blood in the aristocrat, and the sense of doom in
the Calvinist.

G.K. CHESTERTON, *The Innocence of Father Brown* (1911; rept. Harmondsworth: Penguin Books 1950, p.112)

A SCOTTISH CAIN

Had Cain been Scot, God would have changed his doom
Not forced him wander, but confined him home.

JOHN CLEVELAND (1613-58),
'The Rebel Scot'

THE CONCEIT OF THE SCOT

Your proper child of Caledonia believes in his rickety bones

3

that he is the salt of the earth. Prompted by a glozing pride, not to say by a black and consuming avarice, he has proclaimed his saltiness from the housetops in and out of season, unblushingly, assiduously, and with results which have no doubt been most satisfactory from his own point of view . . . He is the one species of human animal that is taken by all the world to be fifty per cent cleverer and pluckier and honester than the facts warrant. He is the daw with a peacock's tail of his own painting. He is the ass who has been at pains to cultivate the convincing roar of a lion. He is the fine gentleman whose father toils with a muck-fork. And, to have done with parable, he is the bandy-legged lout from Tullietudlescleugh, who, after a childhood of intimacy with the cesspool and the crablouse, and twelve months at 'the college' on moneys wrung from the diet of his family, drops his threadbare kilt and comes south in a slop suit to instruct the English in the arts of civilisation and the English language.

T.W.H. CROSLAND, *The Unspeakable Scot*
(London: Grant Richards 1902, pp.11-12)

SCOTLAND AND TRUTH

A Scotchman must be a very sturdy moralist, who does not love *Scotland* better than truth: he will always love it better than inquiry; and if falsehood flatters his vanity, will not be very diligent to detect it.

DR SAMUEL JOHNSON, *A Journey to the
Western Islands of Scotland* (1774)

THE NOBLEST PROSPECT

But, Sir, let me tell you, the noblest prospect which a Scotchman ever sees, is the high road that leads him to England!

DR SAMUEL JOHNSON, quoted in James
Boswell, *The Life of Samuel Johnson* (1791)

A WORSE ENGLAND

Seeing Scotland, Madam, is only seeing a worse England. It is seeing the flower gradually fade away to the naked stalk. Seeing the Hebrides, indeed, is seeing quite a different scene.

DR SAMUEL JOHNSON, quoted in James
Boswell, *The Life of Samuel Johnson* (1791)

KEATS ON SCOTLAND

There was a naughty Boy,
And a naughty boy was he,
He ran away to Scotland
The people for to see –
Then he found
That the ground
Was as hard,
That a yard
Was as long,
That a song
Was as merry,
That a cherry
Was as red –
That lead
Was as weighty,
That fourscore
Was as eighty,
That a door
Was as wooden
As in England –
So he stood in his shoes
And he wondered.

JOHN KEATS (1795-1821), 'A Song about
myself'

THE TRUE CALEDONIAN

I have been trying all my iife to like Scotchmen, and am

obliged to desist from the experiment in despair. They cannot like me – and in truth, I never knew one of that nation who attempted to do it . . . Between the affirmative and the negative there is no border-land with him [the true Caledonian]. You cannot hover with him upon the confines of truth, or wander in the maze of a probable argument. He always keeps the path . . . He cannot compromise, or understand middle actions. There can be but a right and a wrong. His conversation is as a book. His affirmations have the sanctity of an oath.

CHARLES LAMB, Essays of Elia (1823, 1833, 'Imperfect Sympathies')

DEFEATISM

There operates . . . in Scotland . . . a most important sociological law . . . And that is *the petrifying but protective influence of great military defeats on those nations which have nevertheless managed to survive those defeats.* As the Scots themselves are the first to recognise, the whole cultural and political life of Scotland is still attuned, basically, to no later historical period than the mid- or late eighteenth century, except in the neo-Marxist atmosphere of Glasgow and the industrial area, which has entirely leapt the nineteenth century into the present, owing to the challenge of the industrial blight. Cultured Scotsmen today still brood over their defeat by England – under the flattering pretense of 'Union' of the two kingdoms – in the early and mid-eighteenth century.

GERSHON LEGMAN, The Horn Book (New York: University Books 1964, p.365)

INHOSPITABLE SOLITUDE

To describe the wretchedness and comfortless, inhospitable solitude of the country, time and space do not allow . . . To all questions you get a dry 'No'; brandy is the only beverage known, there is no church, no street, no garden, the rooms are pitch-dark in broad daylight, children and fowls lie in the same straw, many huts are without roofs altogether, many are unfinished, with crumbling walls, or just ruins of burnt houses, and even such inhabited spots are but sparingly scattered over the country . . . It is no wonder that the Highlands have been called melancholy.

> FELIX MENDELSSOHN, letter of 15 August 1829 to his family, in Felix Mendelssohn, *Letters*, ed. G. Selden-Goth (London: Paul Elek 1946, pp.57-8)

A MAN CALLED MacGREGOR

MAX. I used to knock about with a man called MacGregor. I called him Mac. You remember Mac? Eh?

Pause

Huhh! We were two of the worst hated men in the West End of London. I tell you, I still got the scars. We'd walk into a place, the whole room'd stand up, they'd make way to let us pass. You never heard such silence. Mind you, he was a big man, he was over six foot tall. His family were all MacGregors, they came all the way from Aberdeen, but he was the only one they called Mac.

> HAROLD PINTER, *The Homecoming* (1965) in *Plays: Three* (London: Eyre Methuen 1978, p.24)

SCOTTISH BALLYHOO

What is this Race whose Pride so rudely burgeons?
Second-rate *Engineers* and obscure *Surgeons,*
Pedant-Philosophers and *Fleet Street* hacks,
With evr'y Quality that *Genius* lacks:
Such Mediocrity was ne'er on view,
Bolster'd by tireless *Scottish Ballyhoo* –
Nay! In two Qualities they stand supreme;
Their *Self-advertisement* and *Self-esteem.*

> ANTHONY POWELL (born 1905), 'Caledonia'

SCOTTISH BRAGS

Parole, parole, nothing but words. The Scots will boast but rarely perform their brags.

DAVID RICCIO (1533-66)

SEEING RED SPOTS

Dukes hunt stags,
While Scotsmen hunt for jobs and emigrate,
Or else start seeing red spots on a moor
That flows to the horizon like a migraine.
Sheep dot the moor, bubblebaths of unshorn
Curls somehow red, unshepherded, unshorn.

Frederick Seidel, 'Scotland', *Men and Women*
(London; Chatto and Windus 1984, p.53)

SHAKESPEARE'S SCOTLAND

MACDUFF. Stands Scotland where it did?
ROSS. Alas, poor country,
Almost afraid to know itself! It cannot
Be call'd our mother, but our grave; where nothing,
But who knows nothing, is once seen to smile;
Where sighs, and groans, and shrieks, that rent the air,
Are made, not mark'd; where violent sorrow seems
A modern ecstasy; the dead man's knell
Is there scarce ask'd for who; and good men's lives
Expire before the flowers in their caps,
Dying or ere they sicken.

WILLIAM SHAKESPEARE, *Macbeth*
(1606; IV.iii.164ff.)

SCOTTISH SENSE OF HUMOUR

It requires a surgical operation to get a joke well into a Scotch understanding.

SYDNEY SMITH (1771-1845), quoted in
Lady Holland, *Memoir* (Vol. 1, Ch. 2)

LAND LEVIATHANS

Some fifty land-Leviathans may be said to possess the Highlands; for the number of smaller heritors, or rather the land which is occupied by them, is comparatively a mere nothing. A few of these are desirous of improving their own estates by bettering the condition of their tenants. But the greater number are fools at heart, with neither understanding nor virtue, nor good nature to form such a wish. Their object is to increase their revenue, and they care not by what means this is accomplished.

ROBERT SOUTHEY, *Journal of a Tour in Scotland in 1819* (London: John Murray 1929, p.209)

AN UNWON CAUSE

You talked of Scotland as a lost cause and that is not true. Scotland is an *unwon* cause.

JOHN STEINBECK, letter of 28 February 1964 to Mrs John F. Kennedy, in *Steinbeck: A Life in Letters*, eds. Elaine Steinbeck and Robert Wallsten (1975; rept. London: Pan Books 1979, p.795)

DANCING LADIES

For vivacity and agility in dancing, none excel the Scotch ladies: their execution in reels and country-dances is amazing; and the variety of steps which they introduce, and the justness of their ear is beyond description. They are very fond also of minuets, but fall greatly short in the performance of them, as they are deficient in grace and elegance in their motions.

EDWARD TOPHAM, *Letters from Edinburgh* (1776, Letter XII)

LAND OF LOST CAUSES

Scotland seemed at a glance ancient, raw, grimy, lush,

 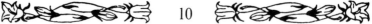

mysterious and mannerly . . . Lost causes abounded.

> JOHN UPDIKE, *Bech is Back* (London:
> Andre Deutsch 1983, p.91)

THE FRONTIER

However often I did it (I have not done it often enough) I could never lose the excitement of seeing SCOTLAND declaimed on the road-sign, and the little line, no wider than a hair-ribbon, painted across the road. It is an astonishing frontier, for, as Valentine [Ackland] said, it is not only the frontier between England and Scotland but the frontier between England and a province of France.

> SYLVIA TOWNSEND WARNER, letter of
> 9 Oct 1953 to Marchette Chute, ed. William
> Maxwell, *Sylvia Townsend Warner: Letters,*
> (London: Chatto and Windus 1982, p.143)

A GOOD DRINK

[H]e was an example of a phenomenon I have observed before: the Celt who becomes a cauldron of turbulent vitality after a couple of whiskies, then subsides into boredom and self-doubt when sober.

> COLIN WILSON, *A Book of Booze*
> (London: Gollancz 1974, p.25)

OBAN

We are now in Oban, which is, as far as I have seen it, the Ramsgate of the Highlands. Only the Scotch having melancholy in their bones . . . being entirely without frivolity build even bathing sheds of granite let alone hotels. The result is grim; and on every lamp post is a notice, Please do not spit on the pavement.

> VIRGINIA WOOLF, letter of 28 June 1938
> to Vanessa Bell

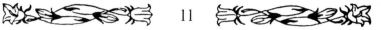

SAVAGE IGNORANCE

A person who has not travelled in Scotland can scarcely imagine the pleasure we have had from a stone house, though fresh from the workmen's hands, square and sharp; there is generally such an appearance of equality in poverty through the long glens of Scotland, giving the notion of savage ignorance – no house better than another, and barns and houses all alike.

DOROTHY WORDSWORTH, *Recollections
of a Tour Made in Scotland A.D. 1803* (London:
David Douglas 1894, Mercat Press 1981,
p.133)

2

BATTLES ANCIENT AND MODERN

DOUGLAS'S DREAM

But I have dream'd a dreary dream
Beyond the Isle of Sky;
I saw a dead man win a fight,
And I think that man was I.

ANON, 'The Battle of Otterburn', Francis
James Child, *The English and Scottish Popular
Ballads* (1882-98, 161C)

A FEUD

Fhairshon swore a feud
Against the clan M'Tavish;
Marched into their land
To murder and to rafish;
For he did resolve
To extirpate the vipers,
With four-and-twenty men
And five-and-thirty pipers.

W.E. AYTOUN (1813-65), 'The Massacre of
the Macpherson'

SCOTTISH BLOOD

Scotland, beloved for the blood of thy sons,
Ah! never again spread the heath-cover'd plain!
Thou stream of the mountain that wand'ring runs,
Ah! never be purpled by faction again.

SIR ALEXANDER BOSWELL (1775-1822),
'On the fidelity of the Highlanders in the
rebellion, 1745-6'

15

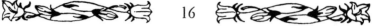

THE ART OF VIOLENCE

Sometimes violence has a reason on the streets – it's political, or religious, or a junkie killing for drugs – either a reason or an excuse. But in the world that I come from, violence is its own reason. Violence is an art form practised in and for itself. And you soon get to know your audience and what it is impresses them. You cut a man's face and somebody asks you, 'How many stitches?' 'Twenty' you say, and they look at you – 'Twenty? Only twenty? Christ, you hardly marked him.' The next time you cut a face you make a bit more certain it will be news.

> JIMMY BOYLE AND TOM McGRATH, *The Hard Man* (Edinburgh: Canongate 1977, p.16)

A BROKEN SPIRIT

To bring a beaten and degraded look into a man's face, rend manhood out of him in fear, is a sight that makes decent men wince in pain; for it is an outrage on the decency of life, an offence to natural religion, a violation of the human sanctities . . . To break a man's spirit so, take that from him which he will never recover while he lives, send him slinking away *animo castrato* – for that is what it comes to – is a sinister outrage of the world. It is as bad as the rape of a woman, and ranks with the sin against the Holy Ghost – derives from it, indeed.

> GEORGE DOUGLAS BROWN, *The House with the Green Shutters* (1901, Ch. 25)

A PARCEL OF ROGUES

Fareweel to a' our Scottish fame,
   Fareweel our ancient glory!
Fareweel ev'n to the Scottish name,
   Sae famed in martial story!
Now Sark rins over Solways sands,
   An' Tweed rins to the ocean,

To mark where England's province stands –
Such a parcel of rogues in a nation!

> ROBERT BURNS (1759-96), 'A Parcel of
> Rogues in a Nation'

DARK LANES

[I]n thrifty Scotland itself, in Glasgow or Edinburgh City, in their dark lanes, hidden from all but the eye of God, and of rare Benevolence the minister of God, there are scenes of woe and destitution and desolation, such as, one may hope, the Sun never saw before in the most barbarous regions where men dwelt.

> THOMAS CARLYLE, *Past and Present*
> (1843, Bk. I, Ch. 1)

FLODDEN

At e'en, in the gloaming, nae swankies are roaming   *young bucks*
   'Bout stacks wi' the lasses at bogle to play,   *peek-a-boo*
But ilk ane sits drearie, lamenting her dearie:
   The Flowers of the Forest are a' wede away.

Dule and wae for the order sent our lads to the Border;
   The English, for ance, by guile wan the day:
The Flowers of the Forest, that foucht aye the foremost,
   The prime o' our land are cauld in the clay.

> JEAN ELLIOT (1727-1805), 'The Flowers of
> the Forest'

A STRANGE MIST

He moved a little the arm he'd thought broken, it wasn't, only clotted with bruises, the dryness had left his throat, he lay still with a strange mist boiling, blinding his eyes, not Ewan Tavendale at all any more but lost and be-bloodied in a hundred broken and tortured bodies all over the world, in Scotland, in England, in the torture-dens of the Nazis in

Germany, in the torment-pits of the Polish Ukraine, a livid, twisted thing in the prisons where they tortured the Nanking Communists, a Negro boy in an Alabama cell while they thrust the razors into his flesh, castrating with a lingering cruelty and care.

LEWIS GRASSIC GIBBON, *Grey Granite*
(1934; rept. in *A Scots Quair*, London:
Pan Books 1982, pp.148-9)

THE WRECKER

What horror, what tragic meaningless horrors, the Wrecker works on man, from without – and from within.

NEIL M. GUNN, *The Other Landscape*
(London: Faber 1954, p.307)

WAR CORRESPONDENTS

The work performed by a newspaper correspondent is most degrading. They can't tell the truth even if they want to. The British public likes to read sensational news, and the best war correspondent is he who can tell the most thrilling lies.

FIELD MARSHAL EARL HAIG (1861-1928),
letter to his sister Henrietta, 5 June 1898,
during Sudan Campaign

FIGHT TO THE END

Every position must be held to the last man: there must be no retirement. With our backs to the wall, and believing in the justice of our cause, each one of us must fight to the end.

FIELD MARSHAL EARL HAIG (1861-1928),
Order of the Day, 12 April 1918

DOMESTIC MURDER

His [Eoghan's] head was viciously wrung back again, and in a horrible silence she [Mrs Strang], with the savage strength of a demoniac, slashed his throat open through the muscles, till the razor scraped on the surface of the bones of the neck. A huge gout of arterial blood spouted on her face, blinding her, and pumped far across the room, splashing on the wall.

J. MacDOUGALL HAY, *Gillespie*
(London: Constable 1914, p.424)

CASTING OUT OF KINGS

When kings cast out and thraw wi' kings,   *fall out, quarrel*
Perhaps about some trifling things,
Some barren island that upbrings
    Some half-starved cattle,
Even clipping of a midge's wings,
    Will breed a battle.

ROBERT HETRICK (1769-1849)

A ONCE-GLORIOUS ARMY

We are shattered, tattered, demented remnants of a once-glorious army. Among us are Princes, and Captains of Armies, Lords of Battles, amnesic, aphasic, ataxic, jerkily trying to recall what was the battle the sounds of which still ring in our ears – is the battle still raging?

R.D. LAING, *The Bird of Paradise*
(Harmondsworth: Penguin Books 1967, p.150)

THE MORAL COMBAT

The moral combat was no mock one, no Valhalla, where warriors are cut to pieces by day and feast by night; but a grim death struggle in which what is worse than death – namely, spiritual death – inevitably awaited the vanquished . . .

DAVID LINDSAY, *A Voyage to Arcturus* (1920;
rept. London: Sphere Books 1980, p.33)

MEMORIES OF WAR

Kings had fallen and nations perished, armies had withered and cities been ruined for this and this alone: that poor men in stinking pubs might have great wealth of memory.

ERIC LINKLATER, *Magnus Merriman* (1934; rept. Edinburgh: Macdonald 1982, p.61)

SLUM VIOLENCE

Battles and sex are the only free diversions in slum life. Couple them with drink, which costs money, and you have the three principal outlets for that escape complex which is for ever working in the tenement dweller's subconscious mind . . . the slums as a whole do not realise that they are living an abnormal life in abnormal conditions. They are fatalistic and the world outside the tenements is scarcely more real to them than the fantastic fairy-tale world of the pictures.

Fighting is truly one of the amusements of the tenements. Nearly all the young people join in, if not as fighters themselves, at least as spectators and cheering supporters.

A. McARTHUR AND H. KINGSLEY, *No Mean City* (1956; rept. London: Corgi Books 1957, p.37)

GLASGOW GANGS

Gangs of louts at every street corner
Full of nothing but *ochiana* . . .
They are hardly persons enough to sustain
Real relations with one another
Any more than billiard balls do.

HUGH MacDIARMID, 'In the Gangs', in *Complete Poems 1920-1976*, eds. W.R. Aitken and Michael Grieve, (London: Martin Brian & O'Keeffe 1978, pp.1325-6)

A FIGHTER

There were a lot of men he [Tam Docherty] knew he couldn't

beat. But there was nobody he wouldn't have fought.

WILLIAM McILVANNEY, *Docherty* (London: Allen and Unwin 1975, p.210)

HORRID BLACK RAINS

The ancient proprietors of the soil shall give place to strange merchant proprietors, and the whole Highlands will become one huge deer forest; the whole country will be so utterly desolated and depopulated that the crow of a cock shall not be heard north of Druim-Uachdair; the people will emigrate to Islands now unknown, but which shall yet be discovered in the boundless oceans, after which the deer and other wild animals in the huge wilderness shall be exterminated and browned by horrid black rains [*siantan dubha*]. The people will then return and take undisturbed possession of the lands of their ancestors.

KENNETH MacKENZIE (17th century), the Brahan Seer, quoted in Alexander Mackenzie, *The Prophecies of the Brahan Seer* (1899; rept. Golspie: Sutherland Press 1970, p.27)

IN SPITE OF AUSCHWITZ AND BELSEN

The broken bottle and the razor
are in the fist and face of the boy
in spite of Auschwitz and Belsen
and the gallows in Stirling
and the other one in Glasgow
and the funeral of John MacLean.

SORLEY MacLEAN, 'The Broken Bottle' (translated from his Gaelic original), *Spring tide and Neap tide* (Edinburgh: Canongate 1977, p.154)

A MEMORY OF VIOLENCE

Bareheaded, in dark suits, with flutes

and drums, they brought him here, in procession
seriously, King Billy of Brigton, dead,
from Bridgeton Cross: a memory of violence,
brooding days of empty bellies,
billiard smoke and a sour pint,
boots or fists, famous sherrickings,
the word, the scuffle, the flash, the shout . . .

EDWIN MORGAN, 'King Billy', *Poems
of Thirty Years* (Manchester: Carcanet 1982,
p.148)

STREET VIOLENCE

I came on a crowd [in Crown Street, Glasgow]. Two young
men were standing in the centre of it, and one of them, who
looked serious and respectable and not particularly angry,
raised his fist slowly every now and then, and, as if
objectively, hit the other man, who stood in silence and never
tried to defend himself. At last an older man said, 'Why dinna
you let the chap alane? He hasna hurt you.' But the serious
young man replied, 'I ken he hasna hurt me, but I'm gaun tae
hurt him!' And with watchful look round him he raised his fist
again.

EDWIN MUIR, *An Autobiography*
(London: The Hogarth Press 1954, p.107)

COMBAT

It was not meant for human eyes,
That combat on the shabby patch
Of clods and trampled turf that lies
Somewhere beneath the sodden skies
For eye of toad or adder to catch.

EDWIN MUIR, 'The Combat', *Collected Poems*
(London: Faber and Faber 1960, p.179)

THE SEVEN DAYS WAR

Barely a twelvemonth after
The seven days war that put the world to sleep,
Late in the evening the strange horses came.
By then we had made our covenant with silence,
But in the first few days it was so still
We listened to our breathing and were afraid.

> EDWIN MUIR, 'The Horses', *Collected Poems*
> (London: Faber and Faber 1960, p.246)

DARIEN

Darien is now a scar on the memory of the Scots, and the pain of the wound is still felt even where the cause is dimly understood.

> JOHN PREBBLE, *The Darien Disaster* (1968;
> rept. Harmondsworth: Penguin Books 1970,
> p.339)

THE SHROUD OF BATTLE

At length the freshening western blast
Aside the shroud of battle cast;
And, first the ridge of mingled spears
Above the brightening cloud appears;
And in the smoke the pennons flew,
As in the storm the white sea-mew.
Then mark'd they, dashing broad and far,
The broken billows of the war,
And plumed crests of chieftains brave,
Floating like foam upon the wave

> SIR WALTER SCOTT, *Marmion*
> (1808, VI, xxvi)

AFTER CULLODEN

As he [Edward Waverley] advanced northward, the traces of

war became visible. Broken carriages, dead horses, unroofed cottages, trees felled for palisades, and bridges destroyed, or only partially repaired, – all indicated the movements of hostile armies.

SIR WALTER SCOTT, *Waverley*
(1814, Ch. 63)

THE UNEMPLOYED

They had come to the end of Lauriston Place, past the fire station, where they were to get on a tram-car to go to tea with Miss Brodie in her flat at Churchhill. A very long queue of men lined this part of the street. They were without collars, in shabby suits. They were talking and spitting and smoking little bits of cigarette held between middle finger and thumb.

MURIEL SPARK, *The Prime of Miss Jean Brodie*
(1961; rept. Harmondsworth: Penguin Books
1965, p.39)

BROKEN

But Annie knew that even if she got another bike it would never be the same. She would always remember Charlie's derisive grin as he looked down at the broken frame, and his scornful words. She knew that something more than her bike had been broken. Nothing would ever be the same again.

FRED URQUHART, 'The Bike' (concluding
sentences) in *The Ploughing Match* (London:
Rupert Hart-Davis 1968)

3

CHARACTERS REAL AND IMAGINARY

ALI ON BURNS

I'd heard of a man named Burns – supposed to be a poet;
But, if he was, how come I didn't know it?
They told me his work was very, very neat,
So I replied: 'But who did he ever beat?'

MUHAMMAD ALI, on his visit to the
Burns Country in 1965

FOUR MARIES

Last nicht there was four Maries,
The nicht there'l be but three;
There was Marie Seton, and Marie Beton,
And Marie Carmichael, and me.

ANON, 'Mary Hamilton', Francis James
Child, *The English and Scottish Popular Ballads*
(1882-98, 173A)

A SELCHIE IN THE SEA

I am a man upon the land,
I am a selchie in the sea,   *seal*
an' whin I'm far from every strand,
my dwelling is in Shool Skerry.

ANON, 'The Great Silkie of Sule Skerry',
version recorded by Otto Anderson in 1938

AMONG THE ENGLISH

A young Scotsman of your ability let loose upon the world

with £300, what could he not do? It's almost appalling to think of; especially if he went among the English.

J.M. BARRIE, *What Every Woman Knows*
(1908, Act I)

A SCOTSMAN ON THE MAKE

My lady, there are few more impressive sights in the world than a Scotsman on the make.

J.M. BARRIE, *What Every Woman Knows*
(1908, Act II)

THE BODIES

In every little Scotch community there is a distinct type known as 'the bodie' . . . The 'bodie' may be a gentleman of independent means (a hundred a year from the Funds) fussing about in spats and light check breeches; or, he may be a jobbing gardener; but he is equally a 'bodie'. The chief occupation of his idle hours (and his hours are chiefly idle) is the discussion of his neighbour's affairs. He is generally an 'auld residenter'; great, therefore, at the redding up of pedigrees. He can tell you exactly, for instance, how it is that young Pin-oe's taking geyly to the dram: for his grandfather, it seems, was a terrible man for the drink – ou, just terrible – why, he went to bed with a full jar of whiskey once, and when he left it, he was dead, and it was empty. So ye see, that's the reason o't.

The genus 'bodie' is divided into two species; the 'harmless bodies' and the 'nesty bodies'.

GEORGE DOUGLAS BROWN, *The House
With the Green Shutters* (1901, Ch. 5)

HOLY WILLIE

But yet, O Lord! confess I must;
At times I'm fash'd wi' fleshly lust;   *irked*

An' sometimes, too, in warldly trust,
    Vile self gets in;
But Thou remembers we are dust,
    Defiled wi' sin.

O Lord! yestreen, Thou kens, wi' Meg –   *last night, knowest*
Thy pardon I sincerely beg –
O, may't ne'er be a living plague
    To my dishonour!
An' I'll ne'er lift a lawless leg
    Again upon her.

Besides, I farther maun avow –   *must*
Wi' Leezie's lass, three times I trow –
But, Lord, that Friday I was fou,   *drunk*
    When I cam near her,
Or else, Thou kens, Thy servant true
    Wad never steer her.

        ROBERT BURNS (1759-96),
        'Holy Willie's Prayer'

NURSING HER WRATH

While we sit bousing at the nappy,   *ale*
An' getting fou and unco happy,
We think na on the lang Scots miles,
The mosses, waters, slaps, and styles,   *breaches, stiles*
Whare sits our sulky, sullen dame,
Gathering her brows like gathering storm,
Nursing her wrath to keep it warm.

        ROBERT BURNS (1759-96),
        'Tam o' Shanter'

BYRON ON BURNS

What an antithetical mind! – tenderness, roughness – delicacy, coarseness – sentiment, sensuality – soaring and grovelling, dirt and diety – all mixed up in that one compound of inspired clay!

        LORD BYRON, *Journal* (13 December 1813)

SIR WILLIAM WALLACE

When he strode o'er the wreck of each well-fought field,
    With the yellow-haired chiefs of his native land;
For his lance was not shivered on helmet or shield,
And the sword that seemed fit for archangel to wield,
    Was light in his terrible hand.

> THOMAS CAMPBELL (1777-1844),
> 'Dirge of Wallace'

BURNS

Society, it is understood, does not in any age prevent a man from being what he *can be* . . . A Scottish Poet, 'proud of his name and country', *can* apply to 'Gentlemen of the Caledonian Hunt', and become a gauger of beer-barrels, and tragical immortal broken-hearted Singer; the stifled echo of his melody audible through long centuries; one other note in 'that sacred *Miserere*' that rises up to Heaven, out of all times and lands.

> THOMAS CARLYLE, *Chartism*
> (1839, 'Laissez-Faire')

A RESPECTABLE MAN

Except that he murdered, Burke [of the Burke and Hare murders] was a sensible, and what might be called a respectable man; not at all ferocious in his general manner, sober, correct in all his other habits, and kind to his relations.

> LORD COCKBURN, *Memorials of his Times*
> (1856, Mercat Press 1977)

TWO HEADMASTERS

    Ane tellt me it was time I learnt to write –
round-haund, he meant – and saw about my hair:
I mind of him, beld-heidit, wi a kyte.   *paunch*

Ane sneerit quarterly – I cuidna square
my savings bank – and sniftert in his spite.
Weill, gin they arena deid, it's time they were.

ROBERT GARIOCH, 'Elegy', *Complete
Poetical Works* (Edinburgh: Macdonald 1983,
p.87)

OLD FISHERMAN

Greet the bights that gave me shelter,
they will hide me no more with the horns of their forelands.
I peer in a haze, my back is stooping;
my dancing days for fishing are over.

The shoot that was straight in the wood withers,
the bracken shrinks red in the rain and shrivels,
the eyes that would gaze in the sun waver;
my dancing days for fishing are over.

GEORGE CAMPBELL HAY (1915-84),
'The Old Fisherman'

NORVAL

My name is Norval; on the Grampian hills
My father feeds his flocks; a frugal swain,
Whose constant cares were to increase his store.

JOHN HOME, *Douglas* (1757, II.i-iii)

THE CALEDONIAN

Bold and erect the Caledonian stood,
Old was his mutton and his claret good;
'Let him drink port', the English statesman cried –
He drank the poison, and his spirit died.

JOHN HOME (1722-1808)

PITY

Not only love for his brother silenced Neil then: he knew that

what Calum represented, pity so meek as to be paralysed by
the suffering that provoked it, ought to be regretted perhaps,
but never despised.

ROBIN JENKINS, *The Cone-Gatherers* (1955;
rept. Harmondsworth: Penguin Books 1983,
p.15)

AN OLD SINGER

[C]rossing the ford to Benbecula, the isle of a thousand lochs,
we came on an old Ossianic singer, of a type supposed to have
long since passed away. He chants tales of such length that
you will go every day for a week to listen to one long tale,
and he will begin to-morrow exactly where he left off to-day,
and his tales are all in verse and traditional, for he neither
writes nor reads. At eighty-seven, still bright and active, he
was to be seen daily out on the machar herding his cattle. And
in the clean white sanded kitchen of his thatched cottage he
sang, but not before he had set everything in perfect order for
the ceremony – these old pagan tales are sacred to the
Isleman.

MARJORY KENNEDY-FRASER, *Sea Tangle*
(London: Boosey and Co 1913, 'An Ossianic
Lay')

ARRIVAL OF MARY QUEEN OF SCOTS
IN SCOTLAND

The ninetein Day of August 1561 Yeirs, betwene seven and
eicht Hours Befoirnone, arryved Marie Quene of Scotland,
then Wedo, with two Gallies furth of France . . . The verie
Face of the Heavin, the Tyme of hir Arryvall, did manifestly
speik quhat Comfort was brocht unto this Countrey with her,
to wit, Sorow, Darknes, Dolor, and all Impiety; for in the
Memory of Man, that Day of the Yeir was nevir sene a more
dolorous Face of the Heavin, than was at hir Arryval, which
two Days efter did so continew. For besyd the Surfece Weitt
and Corruption of the Ayr, the Mist was so thick and dark,

that scarse micht any Man espy ane uther the lenth of two Pair of Butts: The Sone was not sene to schyne two Dayes befoir, nor two Dayes efter. That Fore-wairning gave God unto us; bot alace the most Pairt were blynd.

Befoirnone in the morning;
Weitt wet; *Butts* archery butts

JOHN KNOX, *Historie of the Reformatioun in Scotland* (1586; the Matthew Crawfurd text of 1732)

KNOX VERSUS MARY

'Quhat have ye to do', said sche [Mary Queen of Scots], 'with my Mariage? Or quhat ar ye in this Common-welth?'

'A Subject borne within the sam', said he [John Knox], 'Madem. And albeit I be nyther Erle, Lord, nor Barron within it, yit hes God maid me (how abject that eveir I be in your Eies) a profitabill Member within the sam'.

JOHN KNOX, *ibid*

ON HUGH MacDIARMID

The government decreed that
on the anniversary of his birth
the people should observe
two minutes pandemonium.

NORMAN MacCAIG, 'After his Death',
The White Bird (London: Chatto and Windus 1973, p.12)

A GLASGOW BUTCHER

The butchers of Glasgow have all got their pride
But they'll tell you that Willie's the prince
For Willie the butcher he slaughtered his wife
And he sold her for mutton and mince.

MATT McGINN, 'The Butchers of Glasgow'
(1976)

THE COMMERCIAL VOICE OF THE PEOPLE

The motel – as I see it – is the thing of the future . . . So –
picture it, if yous will, right there at the top of the glen,
beautiful vista – The Crammen Inn, High Rise Motorcroft –
all finished in natural, washable, plastic granitette. Right next
door, the 'Frying Scotsman' All Night Chipperema – with a
wee ethnic bit, Fingals Cafe – serving seaweed suppers in the
basket and draught Drambuie. And to cater for the younger
set, yous've got your Grouse-a-go-go.

> JOHN McGRATH, *The Cheviot The Stag &*
> *The Black Black Oil* (Breakish: West Highland
> Publishing 1974, revd. 1975, p.23)

LAD O' PAIRTS

There was just a single ambition in those humble homes [of
Drumtochy = Logiealmond, Perthshire], to have one of its
members at college, and if Domsie [the schoolteacher]
approved a lad, then his brothers and sisters would give their
wages, and the family would live on skim milk and oat cake,
to let him have his chance.

> IAN MacLAREN, *Beside the Bonnie Brier Bush*
> (1894, 'A Lad O' Pairts')

BURNS ON THE MIND

The *man* Burns exists as a large idea in the national mind,
altogether independent of his literary standing as the writer of
what are pre-eminently the national songs. Our English
neighbours, as a people at least, are much less literary than
ourselves.

> HUGH MILLER, *Essays* (1890, 'The Burns'
> Festival and Hero Worship')

WILLIE WINKIE

Wee Willie Winkie rins through the toon,
Up stairs an' doon stairs in his nicht-gown,

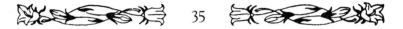
Tirlin' at the window, crying at the lock,   *scraping, calling*
'Are the weans in their bed, for it's now ten o'clock?'

WILLIAM MILLER (1810-72),
'Willie Winkie'

THE WEE MALKIES

Whit'll ye dae when the wee Malkies come,
if they chuck thur screwtaps doon the pan,
an stick the heid oan the sanit'ry man;
when ye hear thum shauchlin doon yir loaby,   *shuffling, hall*
chantin, 'Wee Malkies – the gemme's a bogey!'   *the game's a draw*
Haw, missis, whit'll ye dae?

STEPHEN MULRINE (born 1937),
'The Coming of the Wee Malkies'

BRAND THE BUILDER

The warld ootside
Like a lug-held seashell, sings wi the rinnan tide.

The supper owre, Brand redds up for the nicht.
Aiblins there's a schedule for to price   *perhaps*
Or somethin nice
On at the picters – secont hoose –
Or some poleetical meetin wants his licht,
Or aiblins, wi him t-total aa his life
And no able to seek a pub for relief frae the wife,
Daunders oot the West Sands 'on the loose'.
Whitever tis,
The waater slorps frae his elbuck as he synds his phiz.   *rinses*

And this is aa the life he kens there is?

TOM SCOTT, *Brand the Builder*
(Epping: Ember Press 1975, p.18)

BONNIE PRINCE CHARLIE

The ladies, also, of Scotland very generally espoused the

cause of the gallant and handsome young Prince [Charles Edward Stuart], who threw himself upon the mercy of his countrymen, rather like a hero of romance than a calculating politician.

SIR WALTER SCOTT, *Waverley* (1814, Ch. 43)

SIR ROBERT REDGAUNTLET

Ye maun have heard of Sir Robert Redgauntlet of that Ilk, who lived in these parts before the dear years. The country will lang mind him; and our fathers used to draw breath thick if ever they heard him named. He was out wi' the Hielandmen in Montrose's time; and again he was in the hills wi' Glencairn in the saxteen hundred and fifty-twa; and sae when King Charles the Second came in, wha was in sic favour as the Laird of Redgauntlet? he was knighted at Lonon court, wi' the King's ain sword; and being a red-hot prelatist, he came down here, rampauging like a lion, with commissions of lieutenancy (and of lunacy, for what I ken), to put down a' the Whigs and Covenanters in the country. Wild wark they made of it; for the Whigs were as dour as the Cavaliers were fierce, and it was which should first tire the other. Redgauntlet was aye for the strong hand; and his name is kend as wide in the country as Claverhouse or Tam Dalyell's. Glen, nor dargle, nor mountain, nor cave, could hide the puir hill-folk when Redgauntlet was out with bugle and bloodhound after them, as if they had been sae mony deer. And troth when they fand them, they didna mak muckle mair ceremony than a Hieldandman wi' a roebuck – it was just, 'Will ye tak the test?' – if not, 'Make ready – present – fire!' and there lay the recusant.

SIR WALTER SCOTT, *Redgauntlet*
(1824, 'Wandering Willie's Tale')

KNOX'S SHADOW

John Knox was a native of the town [Haddington] in which I

was born. He was to Scotland what Martin Luther was to Germany. 'Let the common people be taught,' was one of John Knox's messages. His advice was followed and the results were great. The parish and burgh schools of Scotland, and the education given there, are but the lengthened shadow of John Knox.

SAMUEL SMILES, *Autobiography*
(London: John Murray 1905, p.7)

THE HEBRIDEAN SEER

The seer does not inherit his power. It comes upon him at haphazard, as genius or personal beauty might come. He is a lonely man among his fellows; apparitions cross his path at noon-day; he never knows into what a ghastly something the commonest object may transform itself – the table he sits at may suddenly become the resting-place of a coffin; and the man who laughs in his cups with him may, in the twinkling of an eye, wear a death shroud up to his throat. He hears river voices prophesying death and shadowy and silent funeral processions are continually defiling before him.

ALEXANDER SMITH, *A Summer in Skye*
(1865; rept. Hawick; Byway Books 1983, p.97)

OLD WOMAN

And she, being old, fed from a mashed plate
as an old mare might droop across a fence
to the full pastures of its ignorance.
Her husband held her upright while he prayed

to God who is all-forgiving to send down
some angel somewhere who might land perhaps
in his foreign wings among the gradual crops.
She munched, half dead, blindly searching the spoon.

IAIN CRICHTON SMITH, 'Old Woman',
Selected Poems 1955-1980, (Edinburgh:
Macdonald 1981, p.14)

AN EDINBURGH SPINSTER

[I]n many ways Miss Brodie was an Edinburgh spinster of the deepest dye.

MURIEL SPARK, *The Prime of Miss Jean Brodie*
(1961; rept. Harmondsworth: Penguin Books
1965, p.26)

THE FLOWER OF DUNBLANE

How lost were my days till I met wi' my Jessie,
    The sports o' the city seemed foolish and vain,
I ne'er saw a nymph I could ca' my dear lassie,
    Till charmed wi' sweet Jessie, the flow'r o' Dunblane.
Though mine were the station o' loftiest grandeur,
    Amidst its profusion I'd languish in pain;
And reckon as naething the height o' its splendour,
    If wanting sweet Jessie, the flow'r o' Dunblane.

ROBERT TANNAHILL (1774-1810),
'Jessie, the Flower o' Dunblane'

MOTHERLESS CHILD

The mitherless bairn gangs till his lane bed,
Nane covers his cauld back, or haps his bare head; *covers*
His wee hackit heelies are hard as the airn, *iron*
An' litheless the lair o' the mitherless bairn!

WILLIAM THOM (1798-1848),
'The Mitherless Bairn'

4

CULTURAL AFFAIRS

AN AUTHOR'S STATUS

I remember being asked by two maiden ladies, about the time I left the university, what I was to be, and when I replied brazenly, 'An author,' they flung up their hands, and one exclaimed reproachfully, 'And you an M.A.!'

J.M. BARRIE, Margaret Ogilvy (1896, Ch. 3)

TWENTY PIPERS

> To the wedding of Shon Maclean,
>   Twenty Pipers together
> Came in the wind and the rain
>   Playing across the heather;
> Backward their ribbons flew,
> Blast upon blast they blew,
> Each clad in tartan new,
>   Bonnet, and blackcock feather:
> And every Piper was fou,
>   Twenty Pipers together!

ROBERT BUCHANAN (1841-1901),
'The Wedding of Shon Maclean'

BOOKS

On all sides, are we not driven to the conclusion that, of the things which man can do or make here below, by far the most momentous, wonderful and worthy are the things we call Books! those poor bits of rag-paper with black ink on them; – from the Daily Newspaper to the sacred Hebrew BOOK, what have they not done, what are they not doing! – For indeed, whatever be the outward form of the thing (bits of paper, as we say, and black ink), is it not verily, at bottom, the highest act of man's faculty that produces a Book? It is the *Thought* of man; the true thaumaturgic virtue; by which man works all things whatsoever. All that he does, and brings to pass, is the vesture of a Thought.

THOMAS CARLYLE, *On Heroes,*
Hero-Worship, and the Heroic in History
(1841, 'The Hero as Man of Letters')

THE STONING OF SCOTLAND

One lamentable error we certainly have committed, are committing, and, so far as appears, will ever commit. We massacre every town tree that comes in a mason's way; never sacrificing mortar to foliage.

LORD COCKBURN, *Memorials*
(1856, Mercat Press 1977)

SOLITARY THINKING

It seems a grand thing to be able to live apart like a solitary sun that revolves on its own axis, and has no other movement. But this enjoyment of self-culture may be described not less truly in much less flattering terms. We all know how to despise the vices of solitary indulgence – say, solitary drinking; and it is something more than a jest to say that solitary thinking is akin to solitary drinking.

ENEAS SWEETLAND DALLAS,
The Gay Science (1886)

NO COURT, NO COMPOSITION

When the Scottish Court moved south in 1603, a younger generation [of musicians] inherited a fragmented culture that lacked the focus of a royal court to give it direction and

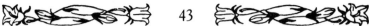

purpose. The result for music was that the art of composition declined.

KENNETH ELLIOTT AND FREDERICK RIMMER, *A History of Scottish Music* (London: BBC 1973, p.41)

EMOTIONAL ACCURACY

The real artist is always *a research man*, and not as people seem to think, an *imitator of recognised forms*. This brings us to accuracy in form, and then we have to ask, accuracy for what, and we immediately realise that it has not even occurred to most people that there is *emotional* accuracy, and that all real precision is *emotional*, in other words human.

J.D. FERGUSSON, *Modern Scottish Painting*, (Glasgow: Maclellan 1943, p.59)

ESTABLISHMENT ART

[T]he *average* artist is often heavily disguised as a fierce revolutionary till he is 'asked in' [by the establishment], which always reminds me of the Salvation Army who used to sing, 'If we can't get in by the Golden Gates we'll climb the garden wall'.

J.D. FERGUSSON, *Modern Scottish Painting* (*Ibid*, p.62)

ARTISTIC CONVICTIONS

Now it seems to be evident that there is a difference between being an artist and having been an artist, and that the word artist strictly applies to the person who *persists in being* an artist.

J.D. FERGUSSON, *Modern Scottish Painting* (*Ibid*, p.103)

THE QUALITY OF PAINT

[I]t is pretty clear that most people have not even thought of *quality* of paint, and that many think that quantity of paint is quality. Quality of paint like quality of line or quality of tone is not a thing that can be fixed. It is the artist's statement in paint of his reaction to form created by the play of light, and is poor or full according to the painter's sensibility and experience of life.

J.D. FERGUSSON, *Modern Scottish Painting*
(*Ibid*, p.107)

DEATH OF WILLIAM MacGIBBON
(*c.* 1695-1756)

At gloamin, now, the bagpipe's dumb,
When weary owsen hameward come;   *oxen*
Sae sweetly as it won't to bum,   *drone*
    An' pibrochs skreed;
We never hear its warlike hum;
    For Music's dead.

Macgibbon's gane! ah waes my heart!
The man in music maist expert;
Wha cou'd sweet melody impart,
    An' tune the reed,
Wi' sic a slee an' pawky art;   *sly*
    But now he's dead.

ROBERT FERGUSSON (1750-74),
'Elegy on the Death of Scots Music'

IMMORTALITY

I . . . intend to immortalise myself by giving to the world a work which shall be read when reading is no more! A work whose fame shall extend from the Taboozamanoo Islands to the last stone of the Mull of Kintyre.

SUSAN FERRIER, letter of 1810 to Charlotte
Clavering

THE GOOD PLACE

Civics as an art, a policy, has thus to do, not with U-topia ['no- place'] but with Eu-topia ['good place']; not with imagining an impossible no-place where all is well, but with making the most and best of each and every place, and especially of the city in which we live.

PATRICK GEDDES, quoted in Philip
Boardman, *The Worlds of Patrick Geddes*
(London: Routledge and Kegan Paul 1978,
p.202)

A NATIONAL ART

I cannot bear to see Scottish writers take their inspiration from English themes. I cannot bear to see our painters paint entirely English subjects. Have they no themes in Scotland; are there no tragedies in the slums of Glasgow, in the mining districts of Lanarkshire and in the Western Islands for men to write about; have our hills and straths lost their enhancement for painters? I say 'No'; but I do say that we want an increase of national sentiment in order to direct the attention of our artists and painters and poets more exclusively to the consideration of national subjects.

R.B. CUNNINGHAME GRAHAM, Speech
at Bannockburn, 21 June 1930, in *Selected
Writings*, ed. Cedric Watts (London;
Associated University Presses 1981, p.90)

CINEMATIC IMAGES

If I raise this matter of images it is rather to give you some idea of how the movie mind works. It has to feel its way through the appearances of things, choosing, discarding and choosing again, seeking always those more significant appearances which are like yeast to the plain dough of the context.

JOHN GRIERSON, *Grierson on Documentary*,
ed. Forsyth Hardy (1946; rept. London:
Faber and Faber 1979, p.22)

COMMERCIAL CINEMA

It [commercial cinema] has given many salutary lessons in critical citizenship, for it has taught people to question authority, realize the trickeries that may parade in the name of Justice, and recognize that graft may sit in the highest places ... It may not have added to the wisdom of the world but it has at least de-yokelized it.

JOHN GRIERSON, *Grierson on Documentary,*
(Ibid, p.56)

TELEVISION AS PARASITE

As for television as parasite, it is a continuously uncomfortable and ugly thing: invading privacy on what the victim, poor devil, has thought on a privileged occasion, exploiting personal emotions and human weaknesses as nastily as the dirtiest of sideshows ...

JOHN GRIERSON, *Grierson on Documentary,*
(Ibid, p.210)

CULTURE AND FREEDOM

If we consider the matter in a proper light, we shall find, that a progress in the arts is rather favourable to liberty, and has a natural tendency to preserve, if not produce a free government.

DAVID HUME, *Political Discourses*
(1752, 'Of Luxury')

THE MOOD OF PIBROCH

To the unpractised ear a pibroch has no form and no melody, and to the accustomed ear it has little more. But it is a mood and a pibroch was something Jock felt almost physically; damp, penetrating and sad like a mist. It enveloped him and pulled at his heart.

JAMES KENNAWAY, *Tunes of Glory*
(1956; rept. Edinburgh: Mainstream Books
1980, pp.29-30)

FOLKSONG RECOGNISED

Folk-song has come into its own of late years. The University of Edinburgh has set its mark on the place assigned to such racial lore by conferring on me the honorary degree of Doctor of Music.

MARJORY KENNEDY-FRASER, *A Life of Song* (Oxford: University Press 1929, p.196)

A SCOTTISH SPIRIT

Suddenly, from out-of-doors, there came a single prolonged, piercing wail, such as a banshee might be imagined to utter. It ceased abruptly, and was not repeated.

'What's that?' called out Maskull, disengaging himself impatiently from Krag.

Krag rocked with laughter. 'A Scottish spirit trying to reproduce the bagpipes of its earth life – in honour of our departure.'

DAVID LINDSAY, *A Voyage to Arcturus* (1920; rept. London: Sphere Books 1980, p.43)

EDIFYING ART

The highest purpose to which painting has ever been applied, is that of expressing ideas connected with Religion . . . The object of a great painter should be, not to invent subjects, but to give a graphical form to ideas universally known, and contemplated with deep feeling.

JOHN GIBSON LOCKHART, *Peter's letters to his Kinsfolk* (1819, Letter XLIX)

BAGPIPES

Their sound is perhaps the only one I know that works in the stomach. It comes like a hard meat, stringy with gristle . . . More than the drab gauds of Caledonia they still flaunt in for Burns suppers and tourism, it steams and twitches in the

cauldron of belonging, the long vault of Celtic exile. Every man who hears it is a king in the blood, returned out of the foreign slime to renew his dead alliance.

> GEORGE MacBETH, *My Scotland*
> (London: Macmillan 1973, p.5)

THE BURDEN

> *A Scottish poet maun assume*
> *The burden o' his people's doom,*
> *And dee to brak' their livin' tomb.*   die
>
> *Mony ha'e tried, but a' ha'e failed.*
> *Their sacrifice has nocht availed.*
> *Upon the thistle they're impaled.*

> HUGH MacDIARMID, 'A Drunk Man Looks
> at the Thistle', *Complete Poems 1920-1976,*
> eds. W.R.A. Aitken and Michael Grieve
> (London: Martin Brian and O'Keeffe 1978,
> p.165)

NO RUINED STONES

There are plenty of ruined buildings in the world but no ruined stones.

> HUGH MacDIARMID, 'On a Raised Beach',
> *Complete Poems 1920-1976, (ibid,* p.425)

EMOTION AND THE BAGPIPES

> And yesterday, and to-day, and forever
> The bagpipes commit to the winds of Heaven
> The deepest emotions of the Scotsman's heart
> In joy and sorrow, in war and peace.

> HUGH MacDIARMID, 'Lament for the
> Great Music', in *Complete Poems 1920-1976,*
> *(ibid,* p.469)

MUSIC WITHOUT MEASURE

Let me play to you tunes without measure or end,
Tunes that are born to die without a herald,
As a flight of storks rises from a marsh, circles,
And alights on the spot from which it rose.

HUGH MacDIARMID, 'Bagpipe Music',
in *Complete Poems 1920-1976, (ibid,* p.665)

THE FACULTY OF INVENTION

The artist cannot attain to mastery in his art unless he is
endowed in the highest degree with the faculty of invention.

CHARLES RENNIE MacKINTOSH,
'Seemliness' (1902), quoted in
Robert Macleod, *Charles Rennie Mackintosh*
(London: Collins 1968, p.101)

NATIONAL ARCHITECTURE

[T]here are many decorative features in Scotch architecture,
which might well be replaced by others of antiquity yet just
because we are Scotch and not Greek or Roman we reject . . .
In fact I think we should be a little less cosmopolitan and
rather more national in our architecture.

CHARLES RENNIE MacKINTOSH,
'Seemliness' (1902), quoted in
Robert Macleod, *Charles Rennie Mackintosh*
(*ibid.*).

NATURALISM

What sort of painters, think you, do the Scotch promise to
become? Why, painters equal to any the world ever produced,
if the national mind be only suffered to get into a national
track, and our artists have sense and spirit enough, however
much they may admire the pictures of other countries, not to
imitate them . . . Let [the Scottish painter] do what was done
by Thomson, and Burns, and Sir Walter Scott, and what

Wilkie, and Allan, and Harvey are employed in doing, – let him walk abroad into nature, and study the history of his country.

HUGH MILLER, *Essays* (1890,
'Criticism for the Uninitiated')

ADVICE TO A WRITER

Study the old Highland tales told by a winter's fire. Study the flow and rhythms of our language. Study most of all the strange cantrips of the human heart.

NEIL MUNRO, letter of 1926 to
Angus MacVicar

THE ART OF PIBROCH

Pibroch is *not* 'Ceol Beag' [light music]. It would, on the contrary, be better to think of it as the only musical form Scotland has given to the world; as an aristocratic art in classical shape and as keeping its distance away from the common and popular. I doubt if it ever was popular, even in the Highlands.

FRANCIS GEORGE SCOTT, 'Pibroch'
Lecture of 1946, quoted in Maurice Lindsay,
Francis George Scott and the Scottish Renaissance
(Edinburgh: Paul Harris 1980, pp.181-2)

RHYTHM OF THE GAELS

It is not surprising then that the Gaels, living as they do so close to nature, base both their folk-songs and their instrumental music on a very definite sense of the importance of rhythm, and give priority to it over the melodic principle. Their melodies in other words grow on, and out of, a pattern of rhythm.

FRANCIS GEORGE SCOTT, 'Pibroch'
Lecture of 1946, (*ibid,* p.176)

THE CALEDONIAN ANTISYZYGY

[Scottish] literature is remarkably varied, and . . . becomes, under the stress of foreign influence and native division and reaction, almost a zigzag of contradictions. The antithesis need not, however, disconcert us. Perhaps in the very combination of opposites – what either of the two Sir Thomases, of Norwich and Cromarty, might have been willing to call 'the Caledonian antisyzygy' – we have a reflection of the contrasts which the Scot shows at every turn, in his political and ecclesiastical history, in his polemical restlessness, in his adaptability, which is another way of saying that he has made allowance for new conditions, in his practical judgment, which is the admission that two sides of the matter have been considered. If therefore Scottish history and life are, as an old northern writer said of something else, 'varied with a clean contrair spirit', we need not be surprised to find that in his literature the Scot presents two aspects which appear contradictory. Oxymoron was ever the bravest figure, and we must not forget that disorderly order is order after all.

G. GREGORY SMITH, *Scottish Literature*
(London: Macmillan 1919, pp.4-5)

THE PIPER

A space he silent stood, and cast his eye
    In meditation upwards to the pole,
As if he pray'd some fairy pow'r in sky
    To guide his fingers right o'er bore and hole;
Then pressing down his arm, he gracefully
    Awak'd the merry bagpipe's slumb'ring soul,
And pip'd and blew, and play'd so sweet a tune,
As might have well unspher'd the reeling midnight moon.

His ev'ry finger, to its place assign'd,
    Mov'd quiv'ring like the leaf of aspen tree,
Now shutting up the skittish squeaking wind,
    Now op'ning to the music passage free;
His cheeks, with windy puffs therein confin'd,

Were swoln into a red rotundity,
As from his lungs into the bag was blown
Supply of needful air to feed the growling drone.

WILLIAM TENNANT, *Anster Fair*
(1812, Canto IV, lxxii-lxxiii)

EXCUSES

The Scots are incapable of considering their literary geniuses purely as writers and artists. They must be either an excuse for a glass or a text for a sermon.

G.M. THOMSON, *Caledonia* (London:
Kegan Paul 1927, p.63)

5

FOOD AND DRINK

EELS FRIED IN A PAN

'And what did she give you, Lord Randal, my son?
    And what did she give you, my handsome young man?'
'Eels fried in a pan; mother, mak my bed soon,
    For I'm wearied wi huntin, and fain wad lie down.

'And wha gat your leavins, Lord Randal, my son?
    And wha gat your leavins, my handsome young man?'
'My hawks and my hounds; mother, mak my bed soon,
    For I'm wearied wi hunting, and fain wad lie down.'

ANON, 'Lord Randal', in Francis James Child,
The English and Scottish Popular Ballads
(1882-98, 12A)

DRIVEN TO DRINK

[T]he living conditions almost anywhere in the industrial belt
[of Scotland] are quite enough to drive any man to drink.

GEORGE BLAKE, *The Heart of Scotland*
(London: Batsford 1934, p.87)

THE OCCUPATION OF DRINKING

Drinking is in reality an occupation which employs a
considerable portion of the time of many people; and to
conduct it in the most rational and agreeable manner is one of
the great arts of living.

JAMES BOSWELL (1740-95), quoted in ed.
Alan Bold, *Drink To Me Only* (London:
Robin Clark 1982, p.140)

A WEAKNESS FOR DRINK

He [young Gourlay] was driven to drink, then, by every weakness of his character . . . For, like all weak men of a vivid fancy, he was constantly framing dramas of which he was the towering lord. The weakling who never 'downed' men in reality, was always 'downing' them in thought.

GEORGE DOUGLAS BROWN, *The House with the Green Shutters* (1901, Ch. 18)

THE WANDERING DRUNK

In Scotland, no occasion of joy or sorrow, of national celebration or traumatic change, is complete without the wandering drunk.

JEREMY BRUCE-WATT, *The Captive Summer* (Edinburgh: Chambers 1979, p.194)

HERE'S A BOTTLE

Here's a bottle and an honest friend
    What wad ye wish for mair, man?
Wha kens, before his life may end,
    What his share may be o' care, man?

ROBERT BURNS (1759-96),
'A Bottle and a Friend'

CHIEFTAIN OF THE PUDDIN RACE

Fair fa' your honest, sonsie face,
Great chieftain o' the puddin-race!
Aboon them a' ye tak your place,
        Painch, tripe, or thairm:
Weel are ye wordy of a grace
        As lang's my arm.

The groaning trencher there ye fill,
Your hurdies like a distant hill,

Your pin wad help to mend a mill
In time o' need,
While thro' your pores the dews distil
Like amber bead.

ROBERT BURNS (1759-96),
'Address to a Haggis'

FREEDOM AND WHISKY

Scotland, my auld, respected mither!
Tho' whiles ye moistify your leather,
Till whare ye sit on craps o' heather
Ye tine your dam,
Freedom and whisky gang thegither,
Tak aff your dram!

ROBERT BURNS (1759-96), 'Scotch Drink'

A PINT OF WINE

Go, fetch to me a pint o' wine,
And fill it in a silver tassie,
That I may drink before I go
A service to my bonnie lassie!

ROBERT BURNS (1759-96),
'The Silver Tassie'

THE VILEST OF BEASTS

O all ye powers of decency and decorum! whisper to them [the ladies] that my errors, though great, were involuntary – that an intoxicated man is the vilest of beasts – that it was not in my nature to be brutal to any one – that to be rude to a woman, when in my senses, was impossible with me – but Regret! Remorse! Shame! ye three hellhounds that ever dog my steps and bay at my heels, spare me! spare me!

ROBERT BURNS, letter of December 1793 to
Elizabeth Kennedy Riddell

SOBER AS A JUDGE

At Edinburgh, the old judges [ie the generation made before 1800] had a practice at which even their age used to shake its head. They always had wine and biscuits *on the bench* . . . Black bottles of strong port were set down beside them on the Bench, with glasses, caraffes of water, tumblers, and biscuits; and this without the slightest attempt at concealment.

LORD COCKBURN, *Memorials of His Time* (1856, Mercat Press 1977)

THE FIRST NIP

Now I don't know if you remember the first time you ever tasted whisky and the tremendous shock to the nervous system that is. In Scotland this usually happens around the age of four – not because your parents give it to you but because there are these parties at New Year.

BILLY CONNOLLY, *Gullible's Travels* (London: Pavilion 1982, p.149)

SCOTCH AND CURRY

The rituals of drink have always fascinated me. The way curry has become a sort of traditional Scottish food after a night of drinking.

BILLY CONNOLLY, *Gullible's Travels* (*ibid*, p.150)

THE MORNING AFTER

I woke up with an aching head
As usual.
I can't remember going to bed
As usual.
My stomach's feeling very queer,
There's a thunderstorm in my right ear,

It must have been McEwan's beer
As usual.

JOHN MURPHY, (as performed by
Billy Connolly), 'As Usual'

A TASTE FOR WHISKY

Whisky, and that of the crudest and most shuddering quality,
is undoubtedly the Scotchman's peculiar vanity. The amount
that he can consume without turning a hair is quite appalling.
I have seen a Scotchman drink three bottles of Glenlivet on a
railway journey from King's Cross to Edinburgh, and when
he got out at Edinburgh he strutted doucely to the
refreshment bar and demanded further whisky.

T.W.H. CROSLAND, *The Unspeakable Scot*
(London: Grant Richards 1902, p.164)

A TOAST TO CIVILIZATION

The proper drinking of Scotch whisky is more than
indulgence: it is a toast to civilization, a tribute to the
continuity of culture, a manifesto of man's determination to
use the resources of nature to refresh mind and body and
enjoy to the full the senses with which he has been endowed.

DAVID DAICHES, *Scotch Whisky* (1969; rept.
London: Fontana Books 1976, p.1175)

GLUTTONY

Than the fowll monstir Gluttony,
Off wame unsasiable and gredy,   *belly*
To dance he did him dres;
Him followit mony fowll drunckart,
With can and collep, cop and quart,
In surfett and excess;
Fully mony a waistles wallydrag   *obese, weakling*
With wamis unwildable, did furth wag,   *stagger*

In creische that did increas; *fat*
'Drynk!' ay thay cryit, with mony a gap,
The feyndis gaif tham hat leid to laip, *hot lead to lap*
Thair lovery was na les. *livery*

WILLIAM DUNBAR (*c.* 1460-*c.* 1513),
'The Dance of the Sevin Deidly Sins'

BOTTLE AFTER BOTTLE

One I could ask has fired his life away
With bottle after bottle to his mouth;
Raw liquor in the turpitude of ditches
While blubbering a sermon on his youth.

DOUGLAS DUNN, 'Drowning',
Barbarians (London: Faber 1979, p.38)

A MAN'S DRINK

When a man takes a drink, he's a man. When ye're teetotal –
Ach! When ye're teetotal ye've got a rotten feeling that
everybody's your boss.

WILL FYFFE, quoted in Albert Mackie,
The Scotch Comedians (Edinburgh: The Ramsay
Head Press 1973, p.45)

THE MEANING OF WHISKY

How did it happen that the Picts passed away, like
Shakespeare's cloud-capped towers and solemn temples,
leaving not a rack behind? As the Maglemosians vanished
before them? And as the Gael is ebbing away after them with
the utter inevitability of an uncorked bottle? Can it be –
horror! – that the white logic of the water of life [whisky]
reflects the face of civilization as the face of an idiot-Narcissus?
That the whole game is not worth putting the cork back for?
Have I stumbled here by chance on what whisky has really
meant to Scotland?

NEIL M. GUNN, *Whisky and Scotland*
(London: Routledge 1935, pp.30-1)

TO KEEP OUT THE COLD

I mend the fire and beikit me about,
Than tuik ane drink my spreitis to comfort,   *spirits*
And armit me weill fra the cauld thairout.

ROBERT HENRYSON,
The Testament of Cresseid (1593)

STRONG WATER

The word *whisky* signifies water, and is applied by way of eminence to *strong water*, or distilled liquor. The spirit drunk in the North is drawn from barley. I never tasted it, except once for experiment at the inn in *Inverary*, when I thought it preferable to any *English* malt brandy. It was strong, but not pungent, and was free from the empyreumatick taste or smell. What was the process I had no opportunity of inquiring, nor do I wish to improve the art of making poison pleasant.

DR SAMUEL JOHNSON,
A Journey to the Western Islands of Scotland (1774)

OATS

Oats, n.s. A grain, which in England is generally given to horses, but in Scotland supports the people.

DR SAMUEL JOHNSON,
A Dictionary of the English Language (1755)

WHISKY FOR ALL

'Whisky. For the gentlemen that like it and for the gentlemen who don't like it, whisky.'

JAMES KENNAWAY, *Tunes of Glory*
(1956; rept. Edinburgh: Mainstream 1980,
p.15)

DILIGENCE ON DRINK

Also I make you exhortation,

Since you have heard the first part of our play,
Go, take a drink, and make collation;
Each man drink to his marrow, I you pray.
Tarry not long, it is late in the day.
Let some drink ale, and some drink claret wine;
By great doctors of physic I hear say
That mighty drink comforts the dull ingyne! *intellect*

> SIR DAVID LINDSAY (*c.* 1490-1555), in
> Robert Kemp's acting version of *The Satire of
> the Three Estates* (London: Heinemann 1951,
> p.37)

A SCRATCH MEAL

In a safe in the kitchen he [Maskull] discovered a bag of moldy oatmeal, which was untouchable, a quantity of quite good tea in an airtight caddy, and an unopened can of ox tongue. Best of all, in the dining-room cupboard he came across an uncorked bottle of first-class Scotch whisky. He at once made preparations for a scratch meal.

> DAVID LINDSAY, *A Voyage to Arcturus*
> (1920; rept. London: Sphere Books 1980, p.33)

HAGGIS

Never eaten without a shudder, spiced, originate in the black mirk of a witchcraft conveniently forgotten, they squat, knotted, horny, reluctant to be moved behind the soiled glass of the delicatessen counter. They seem to crouch, crawl almost. With the alacrity of toads, they approach tables, gathered in strong moments by the clenched hands of aspirant foreigners. Whenever nationals touch them, they wilt, like toadstools.

> GEORGE MacBETH, *My Scotland*
> (London: Macmillan 1973, p.12)

GLORIOUSLY DRUNK

The Scots in early and mediaeval times were known

internationally for their abstemiousness, their severe natural asceticism. How then have they now not undeservedly got a name for addiction to drunkenness, and drunkenness of a particularly senseless kind. Insofar as the aspersion is justified I suggest it is very largely due . . . to the fact that they retained in the benmost recesses of their consciousness, but insistent and demanding, a sense or awareness that there had been a Glory: and they lurched into drunkenness, excessive and senseless drunkenness it might well be, out of despair that they had lost contact with what might have given them dignity, and in the attempt to establish contact and connection.

> FIONN MacCOLLA, *Too Long in This Condition* (Thurso: Caithness Books 1975, pp.20-1)

SCOTCH

And as the worth's gane doun the cost has risen.
Yin canna throw the cockles o' yin's hert
Wi' oot ha'en' cauld feet noo, jalousin' what   *guessing*
The wife'll say (I dinna blame her fur't).

It's robbin' Peter to pey Paul at least . . .
And a' that's Scotch aboot it is the name,
Like a' thing else ca'd Scottish nooadays
– A' destitute o' speerit juist the same.

> HUGH MacDIARMID, 'A Drunk Man Looks at the Thistle', *Complete Poems 1920-1976*, (*ibid*, p.84)

DRINKING IN DIVES

Now, I am not a misogynist by any means. I simply believe there is a time and a place for everything – yes, literally, *everything*. And like a high proportion of my country's regular and purposive drinkers I greatly prefer a complete absence of women on occasions of libation. I also prefer a complete absence of music and very little illumination. I am therefore a strong supporter of the lower – or lowest – type of 'dive' where drinking is the principal purpose and no one wants to be distracted from that absorbing business by music, women, glaring lights, chromium fittings, too many mirrors unless sufficiently fly-spotted and mildewed, or least of all, any fiddling trivialities of *l'art nouveau.*

HUGH MacDIARMID, 'The Dour Drinkers of Glasgow' (1952; rept. in *The Thistle Rises*, ed. Alan Bold, London: Hamish Hamilton 1984, p.208)

THE DEMON DRINK

Oh, thou demon Drink, thou fell destroyer;
Thou curse of society, and its greatest annoyer.
What hast thou done to society, let me think?
I answer thou has caused the most of ills, thou demon Drink.

Thou causeth the mother to neglect her child,
Also the father to act as he were wild,
So that he neglects his loving wife and family dear,
By spending his earnings foolishly on whisky, rum, and beer.

WILLIAM McGONAGALL (1830-1902), 'The Demon Drink'

CRIME AND DRINK

My dear friends, I entreat of you all, for God's sake and for the furtherance of Christ's kingdom, to abstain from all kinds of intoxicating liquor, because seldom any good emanates from it. In the first place, if it was abolished, there would not be so much housebreaking, for this reason: When the burglar wants to break into a house, if he thinks he hasn't got enough courage to do so, he knows that if he takes a few glasses of either rum, whisky, or brandy, it will give him the courage to rob and kill honest people.

WILLIAM McGONAGALL (1830-1902), 'Reminiscences'

A BEER CHASER

Beer does not taste like itself unless it is chasing a dram of neat whisky down the gullet, preferably two drams.

COMPTON MacKENZIE, *Whisky Galore*
(1947; rept. Harmondsworth: Penguin Books
1957, p.21)

SOBRIETY

I have often thought, that it would be a Matter of some Discussion to consider the Effects of Strong Liquors on the human System: with the lower Ranks of Mankind, they are held the prime Vehicles of Happiness, which is the Reason perhaps why our Commons, when they mean to express their being in a State of listless mediocrity, something below Happiness tho' above it's opposite, say they are *sober*.

HENRY MacKENZIE, letter of 26 January
1771 to Elizabeth Rose

CHAMPAGNE SPARKLE

The truest natural-lords and natural-commons division of life lay between those for whom champagne was the natural response to happiness and levity, and those for whom it was a wine only to be consumed on ritual occasions.

ALLAN MASSIE, *One Night in Winter*
(London: The Bodley Head 1984, p.59)

THE LIMBO OF DRINK

In one sense of course all bars were in the kingdom of limbo, the never-never land of those lost girls and boys who had been caught half-way out of their prams. Yet they constituted also a world of double time. On the one hand, time was arrested, drinkers lived in a time capsule; on the other the clock marched inexorably towards the appointed hour when the wire-meshed grill (now framing the gates that beckoned

to the Promised Land) would descend with dull finality, and the worshippers would be driven out of the temple, like mere money-changers, to resume their diurnal tasks.

> ALLAN MASSIE, *One Night in Winter* (*ibid*, pp.65-6)

BARMAIDS

Barmaids are like priests, confessions part of the daily round; surprise is beyond them, often even interest.

> ALLAN MASSIE, *One Night in Winter* (*ibid*, p.69)

FISH AND CHIPS

In every Scottish town and village see
The chip shop shining like the House of God.
It offers more than packages of food:
It shapes the face of the community . . .
Behold the altar with its chromium plate,
Breathe in the fumes of fishy sacrifice;
With pickled eggs, black puddings, greasy pies
There's food for thought for those who lie in wait.

> F. SCOTT MONUMENT (born 1956),
> 'The Chipshoppers'

DRINKING DRAMS

He found that learnin', fame,
Gas, philanthropy, an' steam,
Logic, loyalty, gude name,
   Were a' mere shams;
That the source o' joy below,
An' the antidote to woe,
An' the only proper go,
   Was drinkin' drams.

> GEORGE OUTRAM (1805-56),
> 'Drinkin' Drams'

MINCE AND POTATOES

There was watery mince and potatoes for dinner and nothing at all for tea but pieces-and-jelly.

HELEN W. PRYDE, *The McFlannels*
(London: Nelson 1947, p.19)

HIGHLAND HOSPITALITY

But the central dish was a yearling lamb, called 'a hog in har'st', roasted whole. It was set upon its legs, with a bunch of parsley in its mouth, and was probably exhibited in that form to gratify the pride of the cook, who piqued himself more on the plenty than the elegance of his master's table. The sides of this poor animal were fiercely attacked by the clansmen, some with dirks, others with the dagger, so that it was soon rendered a mangled and rueful spectacle. Lower down still, the victuals seemed of yet coarser quality, though sufficiently abundant. Broth, onions, cheese, and the fragments of the feast, regaled the sons of Ivor who feasted in the open air.

SIR WALTER SCOTT, *Waverley*
(1814, Ch. 20)

LIMITATIONS OF OATMEAL

The common people in Scotland, who are fed with oatmeal, are in general neither so strong, nor so handsome as the same rank of people in England, who are fed with wheaten bread. They neither work so well, nor look so well; and as there is not the same difference between the people of fashion in the two countries, experience would seem to show, that the food of the common people in Scotland is not so suitable to the human constitution as that of their neighbours of the same rank in England.

ADAM SMITH, *The Wealth of Nations*
(1784 edtn, Bk. I, Ch. xi)

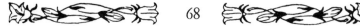

DANGEROUS FEAST

O fain I'd loo ma moujik lass,
    O fain I'd haud her breist –
I've nocht tae haud but a whusky glass,
    A gey wanchancy feast.   *extremely, dangerous*

SYDNEY GOODSIR SMITH (1915-75),
'Ma Moujik Lass'

DRINKING ALONE

O it's dowf tae be drinkan alane, my luve,   *gloomy*
    When I wud drink wi my dear,
Nor Crabbie nor Bell's can fire me, luve,
    As they wud an you were here.

SYDNEY GOODSIR SMITH (1915-75),
'The Steeple Bar, Perth'

SCOTTISH DISHES

Now we are upon the article of cookery, I must own, some of their dishes are savoury, and even delicate; but I am not yet Scotchman enough to relish their singed sheep's-head and haggice, which were provided at our request, one day at Mr Mitchelson's where we dined. The first put me in mind of the history of Congo, in which I had read of negroes' heads sold publicly in the markets; the last, being a mess of minced lights, livers, suet, oat-meal, onions, and pepper, inclosed in a sheep's stomach, had a very sudden effect upon mine, and the delicate Mrs Tabby changed colour; when the cause of our disgust was instantaneously removed at the nod of our entertainer. The Scots, in general, are attached to this composition, with a sort of national fondness, as well as to their oat-meal bread; which is presented at every table, in thin triangular cakes, baked upon a plate of iron, called a girdle; and these, many of the natives, even in the higher ranks of life, prefer to wheaten-bread, which they have here in perfection.

TOBIAS SMOLLET, *Humphry Clinker* (1771)

CONVIVIALITY

Whyles dullness stands for modest merit,
And impudence for manly spirit;
To ken what worth each does inherit,
    Just try the bottle;
Send round the glass, and dinna spare it,
    Ye'll see their mettle.

Oh, would the gods but grant my wish,
My constant prayer would be for this:
That love sincere, with health and peace,
    My lot they'd clink in,
With now and then the social joys
    O' friendly drinkin'.

ROBERT TANNAHILL (1774-1810)
'On Invocation'

6

GAMES FOLK PLAY

THE FOOTBALLER'S FATE

Brissit brawnis and brokin banis,   *torn muscles, broken bones*
Stride, discord and waisite wanis;   *broken homes*
Crukit in eild, syne halt withal –   *old age*
Thir are the bewties of the fute-ball.

> ANON (16th century),
> 'The Bewties of the Fute-ball'

FIXED ON GOAL

Like gods kicking a world about
The players flail at the ball.
Their brains are in their feet,
Their single mind is fixed on goal.

> ALAN BOLD, *Scotland, Yes* (Edinburgh:
> Paul Harris 1978, 'Epilogue')

GUDDLING TROUT

Here he [Andra] scurried and scuttled for all the world like a dipper, with his breast showing white like that of the bird, as he walked along the bottom of the pool. Most of the time his head was beneath the water, as well as all the rest of his body. His arms bored their way round the intricacies of the boulders at the bottom. His brown and freckled hands pursued the trouts beneath the banks. Sometimes he would have one in either hand at the same time.

When he caught them he had a careless and reckless way of tossing them up on the bank without looking where he was throwing.

> S.R. CROCKETT, *The Lilac Sunbonnet*
> (1894, 'Legitimate Sport')

PREPARING FOR SUCCESS

Preparing youngsters for failure is easy; it's preparing them for success that's really difficult.

ALEX FERGUSON, Manager,
Aberdeen Football Club, 1981

THE FIRST BIG SCOTTISH MATCH

I have now been requested by the Committee, on behalf of our Club [Queen's Park], to accept of the Challenge you [Thistle] kindly sent, for which we have to thank you, to play us a friendly Match at Football on our Ground, Queen's Park, at the hour you mentioned, on Saturday, first proximo, with Twenty players on each side. We consider, however that Two-hours is quite long enough to play in weather such as the present . . . Would you also be good enough to bring your ball with you in case of any break down, and thus prevent interruption.

ROBERT GARDNER, letter of 29 July 1868
to Thistle

FOOTBALL IN THE STREET

Shote! here's the poliss,   *police*
the Gayfield poliss,
    an thull pi'iz in the nick fir
    pleyan fi'baw in the street!

ROBERT GARIOCH, 'Fi'baw in the Street',
Complete Poetical Works (Edinburgh:
Macdonald 1983, p.123)

HOPE OVER EXPERIENCE

What distinguishes Scottish soccer, perhaps, is the permanent triumph of hope over experience. Scottish teams have certainly made their mark now and then on the international scene. But in general, they tend to set out on a wave of euphoria and sink without trace . . . Next time, all will be different. It is nearly always next time the Scots are looking for.

CLIFFORD HANLEY, The Scots (1980; rept. London: Sphere Books 1982, p.85)

PRESBYTERIAN ACTIVITY

[T]he game [of golf] is an intensely Presbyterian activity. In golf, you do not play against an opponent. You may play alongside one, but he can't touch your ball or interfere with your swing. You are on your own, one man matching his effort and his conscience against the enigma of life. You may lie about the number of strokes you took to kill a snake in the heather; but you know, and so does the Big Handicapper in the Sky from Whom nothing is hidden.

CLIFFORD HANLEY, The Scots (1980; rept. ibid, p.177)

CURLING

Of a' the games that e'er I saw,
    Man, callant, laddie, birkie, wean,   *lad, youth, chil*
The dearest, far aboon them a',
    Was aye the witching channel stane.   *curling ston*
      Oh! for the channel-stane!
      The fell good name the channel-stane!
      There's no a game that e'er I saw,
      Can match auld Scotland's channel-stane.

JAMES HOGG (1770-1835), 'The Channel Stane'

FOOTBALL AND RELIGION

Football had taken the place of religion in Scotland.

ROBIN JENKINS, A Would-Be Saint (London: Gollancz 1978, p.66)

BRAHMA

I am the batsman and the bat,
    I am the bowler and the ball,
The umpire, the pavillion cat,
    The roller, pitch, and stumps and all.

        ANDREW LANG (1844-1912), 'Brahma'

LIFE AND GOLF

The thing they ca' the stimy o't,
    I find it ilka where!   *every*
Ye 'maist lie deid – an unco shot –   *extraordinary*
    Anither's ba is there!
Ye canna win into the hole
    However gleg ye be,   *nimble*
And aye, where'er my ba' may row,
    Some limmer stimies me!   *rascal*

        ANDREW LANG (1844-1912),
        'A Song of Life and Golf'

GOLF

Golf is a thoroughly national game; it is as Scotch as haggis, cockie-leekie, high cheek-bones, or rowanberry jam.

    ANDREW LANG, *Lost Leaders*
    (London: Kegan Paul 1889, p.56)

THE WEE MAN

up cumzthi wee man
beats three men
slingzowra crackir

    TOM LEONARD (born 1944), 'Fireworks'

THE RITUAL OF RUGBY

[O]nce in alternate years there is a Saturday morning when

Edinburgh is filled with men and women who truly may call the Castle their own and in their bearing not shame its ancient walls. It is not devotion to the gods that calls them in, not some blazing heyday of the Trinity that brings them to worship, nor the inception of a crusade, nor memory, like a phoenix feathered and flowered again, of elder glory that comes in every second year to proper ripeness for a festival. It is not to worship they come, nor to exalt themselves, nor in tears of humility to taste the saltness of the earth, but, very sensibly, to be entertained. And the source of their entertainment is a [rugby] football match between Scotland and England.

ERIC LINKLATER, *Magnus Merriman*
(London: Jonathan Cape 1934, p.145)

PATRIOTIC RUGBY

In this emotional tumult [a Scotland-England Rugby International at Murrayfield, Edinburgh] there is something of the spirit of Bannockburn. It is the annual reassertion of Scottish independence and of a national pride which, although the Scot conceals it successfully in other countries, is more boastful and more aggressive than even the casual arrogance of the English. And the crowd is animated by one fierce, exultant desire: to see Scotland triumph over the old enemy.

R.H. BRUCE LOCKHART, *My Scottish Youth*
(London: Putnam 1937, p.111)

FIGHTING FOR SCOTLAND

I felt I was fighting for Scotland and my true happiness lies in the fact that I did not let Scotland down. My countrymen were looking to me to triumph, and since the referee raised my hand in token of victory I have often thought what I would have done had I failed.

BENNY LYNCH, after winning the World
Flyweight boxing title on 9 September 1935

HIGHLAND GAMES

Little girls breasted only with medals translate
a tune that will outlast them
with formalised legs and
antler arms. High jumpers
come down to earth and,
in the centre
a waddling 'heavy' tries to throw
the tree of life in one straight line.

NORMAN MacCAIG (born 1910),
'Highland Games'

FIGHTING FOOTBALL

Crosshill was a respectable [Glasgow] suburb, but there were
vacant lots scattered about it, chance scraps of waste ground
where the last blade of grass had died, so that in dry weather
they were as hard as lava, and in wet weather a welter of mud.
On these lots teams from the slum quarters of the south side
played every Saturday afternoon with great skill and savage
ferocity. Fouls were a matter of course, and each game turned
into a complicated feud in which the ball itself was merely a
means to an end which had no connexion with the game.
Some of the teams had boxers among their supporters; these
men stood bristling on the touchline and shouted
intimidations at the opposing players.

EDWIN MUIR, *An Autobiography*
(London: The Hogarth Press 1954, p.96)

LIFE AND FOOTBALL

Then strip, lads, and to it, though sharp be the weather,
And if by mischance, you should happen to fall,
There are worse things in life than a tumble on the heather,
And life is itself but a game at football.

SIR WALTER SCOTT (1771-1832),
'Lines on the Lifting of the Banner of the
House of Buccleuch'

A FIERCE FOOTBALLER

He counted was a weil'd wight-man,   *chosen stalwart*
And fiercely at Foot-ball he ran:
At every game the gree he wan,   *prize*
    For pith and speed.
The like of Habbie was na than,   *then*
    But now he's dead.

SIR ROBERT SEMPILL OF BELTREES
(*c.* 1595-1660), 'The Life and Death of the
Piper of Kilbarchan'

IDENTITY CRISIS

I always experience a profound identity crisis about Scotland's
[international football] games. Profound is maybe too
profound a word. Extreme is nearer the mark. For a time
before, throughout and after I have the feeling that my
personal worth is bound up with Scotland's success or failure.

ALAN SHARP, in eds. Ian Archer and
Trevor Royle, *We'll Support You Evermore*
(London: Souvenir Press 1976, p.213)

GOLF ON THE LINKS

Hard by, in the fields called the [Leith] Links, the citizens of
Edinburgh divert themselves at a game called golf, in which
they use a curious kind of bat, tipt with horn, and small elastic
balls of leather, stuffed with feathers, rather less than tennis
balls, but of a much harder consistence. This they strike with
such force and dexterity from one hole to another, that they
will fly to an incredible distance. Of this diversion the Scots
are so fond, that when the weather will permit, you may see a
multitude of all ranks, from the senator of justice to the lowest
tradesman, mingled together in their shirts, and following the
balls with the utmost eagerness.

TOBIAS SMOLLET, *Humphry Clinker* (1771)

SCOTTISH FOOTBALL FANS

We do have the greatest fans in the world but I've never seen a fan score a goal.

> JOCK STEIN, Scotland's Team Manager,
> discussing the World Cup in Spain, 1982

THE ART OF GOLF

The youths in this country are very manly in their exercises and amusements. Strength and agility seems to be most their attention. The insignificant pastimes of marbles, tops, &c. they are totally unacquainted with. The diversion which is peculiar to Scotland, and in which all ages find great pleasure, is golf. They play at it with a small leathern ball, like a fives ball, and a piece of wood, flat on one side, in the shape of a small bat, which is fastened at the end of a stick, of three or four feet long, at right angles to it. The art consists in striking the ball with this instrument, into a hole in the ground, in a smaller number of strokes than your adversary.

> EDWARD TOPHAM, *Letters from Edinburgh*
> (1776, Letter XII)

THE ULTIMATE GOAL

That was the greatest thing he [Dunky] could imagine in the whole world, being picked against England – he'd *die* for Scotland.

> GORDON WILLIAMS, *From Scenes Like
> These* (1968; rept. London: Allison and Busby
> 1980, p.35)

7

GENERAL REFLECTIONS

PIPE DREAMS

Then make I this conclusion in my mind,
Its all one thing, both tends unto one Scope
To live upon Tabacco and on hope,
The one's but smoake, the other is but wind.

SIR ROBERT AYTOUN (1569-38),
'Upone Tabacco'

THE BRAE

As boys we ran up the brae. As men and women, young and
in our prime, we almost forgot it was there. But the autumn of
life comes, and the brae grows steeper; then the winter, and
once again we are as the child pausing apprehensively on the
brig. Yet we are no longer the child; we look now for no new
world at the top, only for a little garden and a tiny house, and
a handloom in the house. It is only a garden of kail and
potatoes, but there may be a line of daisies, white and red, on
each side of the narrow footpath, and honeysuckle over the
door. Life is not always hard, even after backs grow bent, and
we know that all braes lead only to the grave.

J.M. BARRIE, *A Window in Thrums*
(London: Hodder and Stoughton 1889, p.5)

THE OTHER HALF

M'Connachie . . . is the name I give to the unruly half of
myself: the writing half. We are complement and supplement.
I am the half that is dour and practical and canny, he is the
fanciful half; my desire is to be the family solicitor, standing
firm on my hearthrug among the harsh realities of the office

furniture; while he prefers to fly around on one wing.

J.M. BARRIE, *Courage* (1922)

ROMANCE

[R]omance . . . is a revolt against the despotism of facts.

JOHN BUCHAN, *Sir Walter Scott*
(London: Cassell 1932, p.198)

THE GREAT MOMENT

I was especially fascinated by the notion of hurried journeys
. . . We live our lives under the twin categories of time and
space, and when the two come into conflict we get the great
moment. Whether failure or success is the result, life is
sharpened, intensified, idealised. A long journey, even with
the most lofty purpose, may be a dull thing to read of if it is
made at leisure; but a hundred yards may be a breathless
business if only a few seconds are granted to complete it.

JOHN BUCHAN, *Memory Hold-The-Door*
(London: Hodder and Stoughton 1941,
pp.193-4)

MAN AND HIS PLANET

An inconsiderable planet, a speck in the infinite stellar spaces;
most of it salt water; the bulk of the land rock and desert and
austral and boreal ice; interspersed mud, the detritus of aeons,
with a thin coverlet of grass and trees – that vegetable world
on which every living thing was in the last resort a parasite!
Man, precariously perched on this rotating scrap-heap, yet so
much master of it that he could mould it to his transient uses
and, while struggling to live, could entertain thoughts and
dreams beyond the bounds of time and space! Man so weak
and yet so great the chief handiwork of the Power that had
hung the stars in the firmament!

JOHN BUCHAN, *Sick Heart River* (1941; rept.
Edinburgh: Macdonald 1981, p.212)

THE BEST-LAID SCHEMES

But Mousie, thou art no thy lane,   *alone*
In proving foresight may be vain:
The best-laid schemes o' mice an' men
          Gang aft agley,   *go, often, askew*
An' lea'e us nought but grief an' pain,
          For promis'd joy!

Still thou art blest, compared wi' me!
The present only toucheth thee:
But och! I backward cast my e'e,
          On prospects drear!
An' forward, tho' I canna see,
          I guess an' fear!

ROBERT BURNS (1759-96), 'To a Mouse'

AS OTHERS SEE US

O wad some Power the giftie gie us
To see oursels as ithers see us!
It wad frae monie a blunder free us,
          An' foolish notion:
What airs in dress an' gait wad lea'e us,
          An' ev'n devotion!

ROBERT BURNS (1759-96), 'To a Louse'

SAGE ADVICES

Ah! gentle dames, it gars me greet,   *makes, weep*
To think how monie counsels sweet,
How monie lengthen'd sage advices
The husband frae the wife despises!

ROBERT BURNS (1759-96),
'Tam o' Shanter'

DISTANCE LENDS ENCHANTMENT

'Tis distance lends enchantment to the view,
And robes the mountain in its azure hue.
Thus, with delight we linger to survey
The promised joys of life's unmeasured way;
Thus, from afar, each dim-discovered scene
More pleasing seems than all the past hath been;
And every form, that Fancy can repair
From dark oblivion, glows divinely there.

THOMAS CAMPBELL, *The Pleasures of Hope*
(1799, I.7ff)

HEROISM

The Hero is he who lives in the inward sphere of things, in
the True, Divine and Eternal, which exists always, unseen to
most, under the Temporary, Trivial: his being is that; he
declares that abroad, by act or speech as it may be, in
declaring himself abroad. His life . . . is a piece of the
everlasting heart of Nature herself: all men's life is, – but the
weak many know not the fact, and are untrue to it, in most
times; the strong few are strong, heroic perennial, because it
cannot be hidden from them.

THOMAS CARLYLE,
Heroes and Hero-Worship (1841, 5th Lecture)

EARTH HUNGER

What the Scotch call '*a yird hunger*' is a very strong passion.
The tradesman's dream over the counter is of land; and if he
once gets the acres, a single month of them, with 'esquire',
changes his nature. He is a laird, and his dreams are of the
country gentleman. This is the natural aristocracy of land, and
it needs no go-cart to help it.

LORD COCKBURN, *Journals of*
Henry Cockburn (Edinburgh 1874, II, p.171)

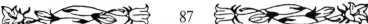

THE DREAD OF DEATH DISTURBS ME

Our plesance here is all vain glory,
This fause warld is but transitory;
The flesh is brukle, the Fiend is slee: *frail, subtle*
  Timor mortis conturbat me.

The state of man dois change and vary,
Now sound, now seik, now blyth, now sary,
Now dansand merry, now like to dee:
  Timor mortis conturbat me.

No state in eard here standis sickir;   *certain*
As with the wynd wavis the wicker,
Wavis this warldis vanitee:
  Timor mortis conturbat me.

WILLIAM DUNBAR (*c.* 1460-*c.* 1520),
'Lament for the Makaris'

MAINTAINING THE PEACE

The wisest policy of nations, except in a very few instances, has tended, we may suspect, rather to maintain the peace of society, and to repress the external effects of bad passions, than to strengthen the disposition of the heart itself to justice and goodness.

ADAM FERGUSON,
Essay on the History of Civil Society (1767)

REAL WEALTH

We men are hypnotized by money but have lost sight of economics – the real functioning of life, in real and energetic health, creating real and material wealth. Real wealth can only be created in a life-efficient environment.

PATRICK GEDDES, *Patrick Geddes in India*
(London 1947, p.70)

THE POSITION OF WOMEN

It is conceivable that every political disability now relating to women might be swept away and that wages become equal for equal quantity and quality of work done by men and women, and yet the position of women be but little really altered unless the existing social and religious institutions and the views incident to the prevalence of these institutions were radically changed.

R.B. CUNNINGHAME GRAHAM,
Selected Writings, ed. Cedric Watts (London: Associated University Presses 1981, p.70)

NOTE OF TRAGEDY

In all things pertaining to his land that move the Scot to his marrow you will observe this note of tragedy, this singing of lost causes, of dead years, of death.

NEIL M. GUNN, *Whisky and Scotland*
(London: Routledge 1935, p.98)

THE TERRIBLE KNOWLEDGE

Already the terrible knowledge of good and evil was in him. He had killed the butterfly.

NEIL M. GUNN, *The Silver Darlings*
(London: Faber 1941, p.100)

THE BULLY

Where all is compulsion and enforcement, it's the bully that rules.

NEIL M. GUNN, *The Silver Darlings*
(*ibid*, p.454)

POWER OF THE TWILIGHT

Many are susceptible to the peculiar power of the twilight, particularly in lonely places . . . Two orders of being, the visible and the invisible, pause on the doorstep of this grey hour, and which is going to advance upon you hardly know. Tension gets drawn out until it is time that is drawn out, so thin, so fine, that its range becomes enormous.

> NEIL M. GUNN, *The Other Landscape*
> (London: Faber 1954, p.13)

A BORN LEADER

A born leader of men is somebody who is afraid to go anywhere by himself.

> CLIFFORD HANLEY (born 1922)
> in conversation

BRED AMONGST MOUNTAINS

Having been bred amongst mountains I am always unhappy when in a flat country. Whenever the skirts of the horizon come on a level with myself I feel myself quite uneasy and have generally a headache.

> JAMES HOGG, letter of 25 July 1802 to Sir
> Walter Scott, in James Hogg, *Highland Tours*
> (Hawick: Byway Books 1981, p.29)

SECOND SELF

I had heart-burnings, longings, and yearnings, that would not be satisfied; and I seemed hardly to be an accountable creature; being thus in the habit of executing transactions of the utmost moment, without being sensible that I did them. I was a being incomprehensible to myself. Either I had a second self, who transacted business in my likeness, or else my body was at times possessed by a spirit over which it had no control, and of whose actions my own soul was wholly unconscious.

> JAMES HOGG, *The Private Memoirs and*
> *Confessions of a Justified Sinner* (1824)

CHANGES OF FORTUNE

All the world wish uninterrupted happiness, a gold[en] age, etc. Were we indulged our wish, adieu to the more noble passions that exalt the human mind. We would sink down to be listless, feeble disspirited creatures; for such passions are only to be roused and invigorated by action and opposition. Man is not made for entire happiness or entire misery; changes of fortune are necessary to preserve him in vigour.

> HENRY HOME, Lord Kames, letter of
> 15 April 1777 to James Boswell (on hearing
> of the death of Boswell's son)

SUPERSTITION

The mind of man is subject to certain unaccountable terrors and apprehensions, proceeding either from the unhappy situation of private or public affairs, from ill health, from a gloomy or melancholy disposition, or from the concurrence of all these circumstances. In such a state of mind, infinite unknown evils are dreaded from unknown agents; and where real objects of terror are wanting, the soul, active to its own prejudice, and fostering its predominant inclination, finds imaginary ones, to whose power and malevolence it sets no limits . . . Weakness, fear, melancholy, together with ignorance, are, therefore, the true sources of SUPERSTITION.

> DAVID HUME, *Essays Moral and Political*
> (1741, 'Of Superstition and Enthusiasm')

SICK MEN'S DREAMS

Survey most nations and most ages. Examine the religious principles, which have, in fact, prevailed in the world. You will scarcely be persuaded, that they are other than sick men's dreams: Or perhaps will regard them as the playsome whimsies of monkeys in human shape, than the serious, positive, dogmatical asseverations of a being, who dignifies

himself with the name of rational.

Hear the verbal protestations of all men: Nothing they are so certain of as their religious tenets. Examine their lives; You will scarcely think that they repose the smallest confidence in them.

DAVID HUME, *Four Dissertations*
(1757, 'The Natural History of Religion')

THE GREATER MIRACLE

When any one tells me, that he saw a dead man restored to life, I immediately consider with myself, whether it be more probable, that this person should either deceive or be deceived, or that the fact, which he relates, should really have happened. I weigh the one miracle against the other; and according to the superiority which I discover, I pronounce my decision, and always reject the greater miracle. If the falsehood of his testimony would be more miraculous, than the event which he relates; then, and not till then, can he pretend to command my belief or opinion.

DAVID HUME, *An Enquiry Concerning Human Understanding* (1758, X, I)

CONTENT

I resolved to make a very rigid frugality supply my deficiency of fortune, to maintain unimpaired my independency, and to regard every object as contemptible, except the Improvement of my Talents in Literature . . . I was ever more disposed to see the favourable than unfavourable Side of things; a turn of mind which it is more happy to possess than to be born to an Estate of ten thousand a year.

DAVID HUME, *My Own Life* (1776)

IMPERFECTIONS

If all mankind were perfectly wise and good, discerning all the proper means of promoting the general happiness of their race, and inclined to concur in them, nothing further would be wanting; no other obligation or bonds than those of their own virtue and wisdom. The necessity of civil power therefore must arise either from the imperfection or depravity of men or both.

> FRANCIS HUTCHESON,
> *A System of Moral Philosophy* (1755)

TOBACCO

A custome lothsome to the eye, hatefull to the Nose, harmefull to the braine, dangerous to the Lungs, and in the blacke stinking fume thereof, neerest resembling the horrible Stigian smoke of the pit that is bottomelesse.

> JAMES I, *A Counterblaste to Tobacco* (1604)

THE MONSTROUS REGIMENT

To promote a woman to bear rule, superiority, dominion, or empire, above any realm, nation or city, is repugnant to nature, contumely to God, a thing most contrarious to his revealed will and approved ordinance; and, finally, it is the subversion of all equity and justice.

> JOHN KNOX, *The First Blast of the Trumpet*
> *Against the Monstrous Regiment of Women*
> (1558, opening sentence)

SCHIZOPHRENIA

In using the term schizophrenia, I am not referring to any condition that I suppose to be mental rather than physical, or to an illness, like pneumonia, but to a label that some people pin on other people under certain social circumstances.

> R.D. LAING, *The Politics of Experience*
> (Harmondsworth: Penguin Books 1967, p.86)

THE END OF THE ROAD

> Keep right on to the end of the Road,
>   Keep right on to the end.
> If the way be rough, let your heart be strong,
>   Keep right on round the bend.
> Though you're tired and weary, still journey on
>   Till you come to that happy abode,
> Where all you've loved and been longing for
>   Will be there – at the End of the Road!

> SIR HARRY LAUDER (1870-1950),
> 'The End of the Road'

THE CANNY SCOT

If folk think I'm mean, they'll no' expect too much.

> SIR HARRY LAUDER, quoted in Albert
> Mackie, *The Scotch Comedians* (Edinburgh:
> The Ramsay Head Press 1973, p.32)

CURSE OF SCEPTICISM

One of the greatest curses of a sceptical philosophy, is that, by leaving no object upon which the disinterested affections may exercise themselves, it is apt to cause the minds of mankind to be too exclusively taken up about the paltry gratifications of the personal feelings. When the true ornaments of our nature are forgotten, Pride and Vanity must become the arbiters of human life.

> JOHN GIBSON LOCKHART,
> *Peter's Letters to his Kinsfolk* (1819, Letter XL)

A GREATER CHRIST

> A greater Christ, a greater Burns, may come.
> The maist they'll dae is to gi'e bigger pegs
> To folly and conceit to hank their rubbish on.

They'll cheenge folks' talk but no their natures, fegs!

HUGH MacDIARMID, 'A Drunk Man Looks at the Thistle', *Complete Poems 1920-1976*, eds. W.R. Aitken and Michael Grieve (London: Martin Brian and O'Keeffe 1978, p.86)

NO HALF-WAY HOUSE

I'll ha'e nae hauf-way hoose, but aye be whaur
Extremes meet – it's the only way I ken
To dodge the curst conceit o' bein' richt
That damns the vast majority o' men.

HUGH MacDIARMID, 'A Drunk Man Looks at the Thistle', (*ibid*, p.87)

TO BE YOURSELVES

And let the lesson be – to be yersel's,
Ye needna fash gin it's to be ocht else.   *worry, if*
To be yersel's – and to mak' that worth bein'.
Nae harder job to mortals has been gi'en.

HUGH MacDIARMID, 'A Drunk Man Looks at the Thistle', (*ibid*, p.107)

ALL THE WORLD

He's no a man ava',
And lacks a proper pride,
Gin less than a' the warld   *if*
Can ser' him for a bride!

HUGH MacDIARMID, 'A Drunk Man Looks at the Thistle', (*ibid*, p.114)

THE LONE SHIELING COMPLEX

As a girl Caroline Macdonald had suffered from the Lone Shieling complex.

COMPTON MacKENZIE, *The Monarch of the Glen* (1941; rept. Harmondsworth: Penguin Books 1959, p.11)

MATERIALISM

There are certain interests which the world supposes every man to have, and which therefore are properly enough termed worldly; but the world is apt to make an erroneous estimate: ignorant of the dispositions which constitute our happiness or misery, they bring to an undistinguished scale the means of the one, as connected with power, wealth, or grandeur, and of the other with their contraries. Philosophers and poets have often protested against this decision; but their arguments have been despised as declamatory, or ridiculed as romantic.

HENRY MacKENZIE, *The Man of Feeling* (1771, Ch. 12)

A LACK OF LAUGHTER

In Scotland we can be very bitter in our Wrath, seldom jocose in our Satire; We can lash an Adversary but want the Art of laughing at him, which is frequently the severer Revenge of the two.

HENRY MacKENZIE, letter of 11 October 1770 to Elizabeth Rose

ENDLESS LIFE

The life of every man is an endlessly repeated performance of the life of man.

EDWIN MUIR, *An Autobiography* (London: The Hogarth Press 1954, p.49)

TURNING ALWAYS

There is a road that turning always
Cuts off the country of Again.
Archers stand there on every side
And as it runs time's deer is slain,
And lies where it has lain.

EDWIN MUIR, 'The Road', *Collected Poems*
(London: Faber and Faber 1960, p.61)

THE DEAD

I try to realise heaven to myself, and I cannot do it. The more
I think of it, the less I am able to feel that those who have left
us can start up at once into a heartless beatitude without
caring for our sorrow. Do they sleep until the Great day? Or
does time so cease for them that it seems but a matter of hours
and minutes till we meet again? God who is Love cannot give
immortality and annihilate affection; that surely, at least, we
must take for granted – as sure as they live they live to love
us. Human nature in the flesh cannot be more faithful, more
tender, than the purified human soul in heaven. Where, then,
are they, those who have gone before us? Some people say
around us, still knowing all that occupies us; but that is an idea
I cannot entertain either. It would not be happiness but pain to
be beside those we love yet unable to communicate with
them, unable to make ourselves known.

MARGARET OLIPHANT, *Autobiography*
(1899; rept. Leicester: University Press 1974,
p.93)

FAITH

I am persuaded, that the unjust *live by faith* as well as the *just*;
that, if all belief could be laid aside, piety, patriotism,
friendship, parental affection, and private virtue, would appear
as ridiculous as knight-errantry; and that the pursuits of
pleasure, of ambition, and of avarice, must be grounded upon

belief, as well as those that are honourable or virtuous.

THOMAS REID, *An Inquiry into the Human Mind* (1764)

LUCY ASHTON'S SONG

Look not thou on beauty's charming,
Sit thou still when kings are arming,
Taste not when the wine-cup glistens,
Speak not when the people listens,
Stop thine ear against the singer,
From the red gold keep thy finger;
Vacant heart and hand and eye,
Easy live and quiet die.

SIR WALTER SCOTT,
The Bride of Lammermoor (1819)

FOUR DISTINCT STATES

There are four distinct states which mankind passes through. 1st the age of Hunters; 2nd, the age of Shepherds; 3rd, the age of Agriculture; 4th, the age of Commerce.

ADAM SMITH, Lecture Notes for 24 December 1762

PARSIMONY

Parsimony and not industry is the immediate cause of the increase of capital. Industry, indeed, provides the subject which parsimony accumulates. But whatever industry might acquire, if parsimony did not save and store up, the capital would never be the greater.

Parsimony, by increasing the fund which is destined for the maintenance of productive hands, tends to increase the number of those hands whose labour adds to the value of the subject upon which it is bestowed. It tends therefore to increase the exchangeable value of the annual produce of the

land and labour of the country. It puts into motion an additional quantity of industry, which gives an additional value to the annual produce.

ADAM SMITH, *The Wealth of Nations*
(1776, Vol. 1)

DIVISION OF LABOUR

This division of labour, from which so many advantages are derived, is not originally the effect of any human wisdom, which foresees and intends that general opulence to which it gives occasion. It is the necessary, though very slow and gradual consequence of a certain propensity in human nature which has in view no such extensive utility; the propensity to truck, barter, and exchange one thing for another.

ADAM SMITH, *The Wealth of Nations*
(1784 edtn)

AN INHUMAN PRIDE

A deer looks through you to the other side,
and what it is and sees is an inhuman pride.

IAIN CRICHTON SMITH, 'Deer on the
High Hills', *Selected Poems 1955-1980*
(Edinburgh: Macdonald 1981, p.42)

TRUE HAPPINESS

If there be such a thing as true happiness on earth, I enjoy it.

TOBIAS SMOLLETT, *Roderick Random*
(1748, Ch. LXIX)

SUFFERING

How can you deal with the problem of suffering if everybody conspires to estrange you from suffering?

MURIEL SPARK, *The Only Problem*
(London: Bodley Head 1984, p.64)

A CHANGE OF MIND

For my part, I look back to the time when I was a Socialist with something like regret. I have convinced myself (for the moment) that we had better leave these great changes to what we call great blind forces: their blindness being so much more perspicacious than the little, peering, partial eyesight of men.

ROBERT LOUIS STEVENSON, *Virginibus Puerisque* (1881, 'Crabbed Age and Youth')

BROTHERHOOD

For people are not most conscious of brotherhood when they continue languidly together in one creed, but when, with some doubt, with some danger perhaps, and certainly not without some reluctance, they violently break with the tradition of the past, and go forth from the sanctuary of their fathers to worship under the bare heaven. A new creed, like a new country, is an unhomely place of sojourn; but it makes men lean on one another and join hands.

ROBERT LOUIS STEVENSON, *Familiar Studies of Men and Books* (1882, 'Knox and His Relations to Women')

A PROFOUND DUPLICITY

Hence it came about that I concealed my pleasures; and that when I reached years of reflection, and began to look round me, and take stock of my progress and position in the world, I stood already committed to a profound duplicity of life. Many a man would have even blazoned such irregularities as I was guilty of; but from the high views that I had set before me, I regarded and hid them with an almost morbid sense of shame ... Though so profound a double-dealer, I was in no sense a hypocrite; both sides of me were in dead earnest ... I thus drew steadily nearer to that truth, by whose partial discovery I have been doomed to such a dreadful shipwreck: that man is not truly one, but truly two ... It was on the moral side, and

in my own person, that I learned to recognize the thorough and primitive duality of man; I saw that, of the two natures that contended in the field of my consciousness, even if I could rightly be said to be either, it was only because I was radically both.

ROBERT LOUIS STEVENSON,
The Strange Case of Dr Jekyll and Mr Hyde (1886,
'Henry Jekyll's Full Statement of the Case')

INTELLECTUAL EXERCISE

To be wholly devoted to some intellectual exercise is to have succeeded in life . . .

ROBERT LOUIS STEVENSON,
Weir of Hermiston (1896, Ch. 2)

REQUIEM

This be the verse you grave for me:
Here he lies where he longed to be;
Home is the sailor, home from sea,
*   And the hunter home from the hill.*

ROBERT LOUIS STEVENSON (1850-94),
'Requiem'

AUTUMN

The western sun withdraws the shortened day;
And humid evening, gliding o'er the sky,
In her chill progress, to the ground condensed
The vapors throws. Where creeping waters ooze,
Where marshes stagnate, and where rivers wind,
Cluster the rolling fogs, and swim along
The dusky-mantled lawn. Meanwhile the moon,
Full-orbed and breaking through the scattered clouds,
Shows her broad visage in the crimsoned east.

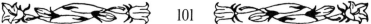
Turned to the sun direct, her spotted disk
(Where mountains rise, umbrageous dales descend,
And caverns deep, as optic tube descries)
A smaller earth, gives all his blaze again,
Void of its flame, and sheds a softer day.

JAMES THOMSON, *The Seasons*
(1730, 'Autumn')

LIFE IS BUT A DREAM

For life is but a dream whose shapes return,
  Some frequently, some seldom, some by night
And some by day, some night and day: we learn,
  The while all change and many vanish quite,
In their recurrence with recurrent changes
A certain seeming order; where this ranges
  We count things real; such is memory's night.

JAMES THOMSON |B.V.| (1834-82),
'The City of Dreadful Night' (Canto I)

THE CITY OF DREADFUL NIGHT

The City is of Night, but not of sleep;
  There sweet sleep is not for the weary brain;
The pitiless hours like years and ages creep,
  A night seems termless hell. This dreadful strain
Of thought and consciousness which never ceases,
Or which some moments' stupor but increases,
  This, worse than woe, makes wretches there insane.

They leave all hope behind who enter there:
  One certitude while sane they cannot leave,
One anodyne for torture and despair;
  The certitude of Death, which no reprieve
Can put off long; and which, divinely tender,
But waits the outstretched hand to promptly render
  That draught whose slumber nothing can brave.

JAMES THOMSON |B.V.| (1834-82),
'The City of Dreadful Night' (Canto I)

A PIPE, A BOOK

Give a man a pipe he can smoke,
  Give a man a book he can read;
And his home is bright with a calm delight,
  Though the rooms be poor indeed.

JAMES THOMSON [B.V.] (1834-82),
'Sunday Up the River'

SCOTSMEN AND ENGLISHMEN

[T]here is nocht twa natiouns under the firmament that are
mair contrar and different fra otheris nor is Inglis men and
Scottis men, quhoubeit that thay be within ane ile, and
nichtbours, and of ane langage. For Inglis men are subtil, and
Scottis men are facile. Inglis men are ambitious in prosperity,
and Scottis men are humain in prosperity. Inglis men are
hummil quhen thay are subjeckit be force and violence, and
Scottis men are furious quhen thay are violently subjeckit.
Inglis men are cruel quhen thay get victory, and Scottis men
are merciful quhen thay get victory. And to conclude, it is
impossible that Scottis men and Inglis men can remain in
concord under ane monarchy or ane prince, because ther
naturis and conditiouns are as indefferent as is the nature of
scheip and wolvis.

ROBERT WEDDERBURN,
The Complaynt of Scotland (1549, Ch. 13)

HAND-MADE

When I was a wee girl [in Glasgow] if you said that
something looked 'hand-made' it was the greatest insult you
could hurl at the disparaged article. To be exactly the same as
everyone else was the look that was coveted, and great was
the anguish suffered by children whose mothers had to make
do and mend from anything which came to hand.

MOLLY WEIR, *Shoes Were For Sunday*
(1970; rept. London: Pan Books 1973, p.78)

IN THE GRAVE

              I understood this prison;
A symbol of the womb, it was the presage
Of my new birth. No midwife would be needed
For this confinement; precocious embryo,
I should prick the pregnant bubble. These stones would vanish,
The prisoner escaping with the prison.

ANDREW YOUNG, *Out of the World and Back*
(London: Rupert Hart-Davis 1961, p.12)

8

LANGUAGE

A SCOTCH WORD

He had wanted a Scotch word that would signify how many people were in church, and it was on the tip of his tongue but would come no farther.

J.M. BARRIE, *Sentimental Tommy*
(London: Cassell 1896, p.437)

HOGMANAY IN GLASGOW

How exhilarating it was to sojourn once more in Glasgow, that charming citadel of tradition and culture. By a happy chance my arrival coincided with the ancient and picturesque Festival of Hogmanay or, as it is known in the native patois, RA BIG BOOZE-UP.

It was my good fortune to meet with a gentleman who invited me to accompany him to the sacred Hogmaniacal rites at a residence in the remote Southern terrain of the city called RASOOSIDE.

When I suggested that it might be expedient to engage a taxicab my companion mentioned a lady's name. 'NORAH!' he said, 'NORAHBLIDDICHANCE'. Before I could question him as to the lady's identity he made certain obscure references to snow and the Yukon . . . 'SNOWFAUR', he stated, 'YUKONHOOFIT'.

STANLEY BAXTER AND
ALEX MITCHELL, *Parliamo Glasgow*
(Edinburgh: Paul Harris, 1982, p.27)

AWKWARD ENGLISH

In a word, we handle English, as a person who cannot fence

handles a sword; continually afraid of hurting ourselves with it, or letting it fall, or making some awkward motion that shall betray our ignorance . . .

JAMES BEATTIE (1735-1803), quoted in
Sir William Forbes, *Life and Writings of Beattie*
(II, p.17)

A PURE SILENCE

Perhaps language, which seems to be among man's greatest gifts, is really a source of discord, confusion, and death. Perhaps in the end, in that good age when the lion shall lie down with the lamb, there will be no need of speech. Men and beasts, birds and fish and plants, will converse with each other in a pure silence beyond utterance; the body's gestures, like a dance, will say everything.

GEORGE MacKAY BROWN, *Time in a Red Coat* (London: Chatto and Windus 1984, p.104)

PURITY OF LANGUAGE

We who deal in words must strive to keep language pure and wholesome; and it is hard work, as hard almost as digging a stony field with a blunt spade.

GEORGE MacKAY BROWN, *Time in a Red Coat* (*ibid*, p.104)

LALLANS

In days when mankind were but callans;   *striplings*
At grammar, logic, an' sic talents,
They took nae pains their speech to balance,
    Or rules to gie;   *give*
But spak their thoughts in plain, braid Lallans,   *broad, Lowlands*
    Like you or me.

ROBERT BURNS (1759-96),
'To William Simpson of Ochiltree'

ENGLISH A FOREIGN LANGUAGE

Since we began to affect speaking a foreign language, which the English dialect is to us, humour, it must be confessed, is less apparent in conversation.

ALEXANDER CARLYLE, *Autobiography*,
ed. John Hill Burton (1860; rept. Edinburgh:
T.N. Foulis 1910, p.232)

THAT WHICH WORKS

The proof of the pudding is in the eating, and the best language is that which *works*.

DAVID DAICHES, Introduction to the
second edtn. of Hugh MacDiarmid,
A Drunk Man Looks at the Thistle (Glasgow:
Caledonian Press 1953)

MANY A TONGUE

Sae let nae daft presumptuous loon
Wha's plaid's a stiflin' word-cocoon
Preach Lallans tae me, late an' soon.
 There's mony a sang
In mony a tongue aneath the moon –
 An nane is wrang!

GAVIN EWART, 'A Wee Sang for St
Andrew's Day', *The Collected Ewart 1933-1980*
(London: Hutchinson 1980, p.383)

MOTHER TONGUE

Nor will the search be hard or long:
For tho' 'tis true that Mither-tongue
Has had the melancholy fate
To be neglekit by the great,
She still has fun an open door   *found*
Amang the uncurriptit poor,

Wha be na weent to treat wi' scorn   *wont*
A gentlewoman bred and born,
But bid her, thoch in tatters drest,
A hearty welcome to their best.

    There aft on benmaist bink she sits,   *innermost*
bench
And sharps the edge of cuintry wits,   *country*
Wi' routh of gabby saws, an' says,   *plenty*
An' jokes, an' gibes of uther days:
That gi'e si'k gust to rustic sport   *such*
And gar the langsome night leuk short.   *make*

            ALEXANDER GEDDES, (1737-1802),
            'Epistle to the President, Vice-Presidents,
            and Members of the Scottish Society of
            Antiquaries; On Being Chosen a
            Correspondent Member'

VERBS OF THE SEA

The great verbs of the sea
Come down on us in a roar.
What shall I answer for?

            W.S. GRAHAM, *The Nightfishing*
            (London: Faber 1955, 'Letter VI')

LINGUISTIC PHILOSOPHY

Nothing is more usual than for philosophers to encroach upon
the province of grammarians; and to engage in disputes of
words, while they imagine that they are handling
controversies of the deepest importance and concern.

            DAVID HUME, *An Enquiry Concerning the
            Principles of Morals* (1751, App. IV)

THE DEAR AULD LALLANS

Och, I wish you hadn't come right now;
You've put me off my balance.

I was just translating my last wee poem
Into the dear auld Lallans.

ALAN JACKSON, 'A Scotch poet speaks',
The Grim Wayfarer (London: Fulcrum 1969,
p.40)

SUSPECT WORDS

Words are so suspect, as we know. Much as I've tried them
before the horrid little Scot locked up inside has betrayed my
best intentions.

JAMES KENNAWAY, letter of 1 March 1964,
in Susan Kennaway, *The Kennaway Papers*
(London: Jonathan Cape 1981, pp.90-1)

LINGUISTIC CHAUVINISM

All modes of speech are valid – upper-class, middle-class,
working-class, from whatever region: linguistic chauvinism is
a drag, pre-judging people just because they speak 'rough' or
with the accent of another region, or equally, pre-judging
people just because they speak 'posh'.

TOM LEONARD, *Intimate Voices*
(Newcastle: Galloping Dog Press 1984, p.95)

FEEDING THE FIVE THOUSAND

There wis a dail of gerss i the place, an the men lay doun, like
five thousand o them. Syne Jesus tuik the laifs, gae thenks, an
haufed them amang the fowk as they lay on the swaird, an the
like wi the fishes; an ilkane gat as muckle as he wantit. Whan
they hed aa haen their sairin, he said til his disciples, 'Gether
up the owrecome pieces, sae at nocht be waistit.' They did as
they war bidden; an the stoos o the five bear laifs left owre bi
them at hed etten fu'd twal creels.

Whan they saw whattan a miracle he hed wrocht, the fowk
begoud sayin, 'This is the Prophet at wis tae come intil the
warld, atweill!'

Syne Jesus, seein at they war ettlin tae come an cairrie him awà sting and ling tae mak him King, gaed awà back tae the hill, himlane.

W.L. LORIMER, *The New Testament in Scots* (Edinburgh: Southside 1983, p.169)

LIBERATION OF THE DORIC

We have been enormously struck by the resemblance – the moral resemblance – between Jamieson's Etymological Dictionary of the Scottish language and James Joyce's *Ulysses*. A *vis comica* that has not yet been liberated lies bound by desuetude and misappreciation in the recesseses of the Doric: and its potential uprising would be no less prodigious, uncontrollable, and utterly at variance with conventional morality than was Joyce's tremendous outpouring.

HUGH MacDIARMID, 'A Theory of Scots Letters' (1923; rept. in *The Thistle Rises*, ed. Alan Bold, London: Hamish Hamilton 1984, p.129)

NAMES FOR NAMELESS THINGS

It's soon', no' sense, that faddoms the herts o' men,
And by my sangs the rouch auld Scots I ken
E'en herts that ha'e nae Scots 'll dirl richt thro'
As nocht else could – for here's a language rings
Wi' datchie sesames, and names for nameless things.   secret

HUGH MacDIARMID, 'Gairmscoile', *Collected Poems 1920-1976*, eds. W.R. Aitken and Michael Grieve (London: Martin Brian and O'Keeffe 1978, p.74).

MASTERY OF LANGUAGE

It is wonderful what a weight of out-of-the-way terminology one can carry along successfully in the current of a genuine poetic impulse or overcome by sheer concentration of effort towards finding its ideal use. It is along these lines and no other that Scots can be profitably used and no one should attempt to use it unless he finds English incapable of what he wishes to express . . . translating English or other poetry into Scots is hopeless if the method is only to hunt out terms in Scots which have some correspondence in *mere meaning* to those in the poem in question. In other words you must master the language *first*. Poetry cannot be written in any language save by a master of it.

> HUGH MacDIARMID, letter of 13 April 1926
> to J.K. Annand, in *The Letters of Hugh
> MacDiarmid*, ed. Alan Bold (London:
> Hamish Hamilton 1984, pp.362-3)

A GLOSS ON LANGUAGE

'Tis pity that the [Scots] Language . . . will probably soon become so antiquated as not to be understood: Glossaries do but very ill supply this Defect; it is a cool Operation to stop in the midst of a Sentiment or Description to scrutinise the Sense of a Vocable.

> HENRY MacKENZIE, letter of 17 August
> 1775 to Elizabeth Rose

GAELIC

No poetry is translatable, and the more verse approximates to poetry the more untranslatable it is. Gaelic poetry is especially difficult for many reasons: Gaelic is so much outside the Western European traditions; it has so little Latin/Greek/Romance vocabulary (although it has some), unlike English, French, etc; by far the primary sensuousness of Gaelic poetry has always been sound; Gaelic is a mid-European language and therefore Scots is too Teutonic or Nordic for it and English is too much affected by its huge accretions of Romance vocabulary; the ratio of quantity of long and short vowels is much greater in Gaelic than in English or Scots.

> SORLEY MacLEAN, letter of 19 June 1979
> to Alan Bold

CELTIC TWILIGHT

The last tragedy for broken nations is not the loss of power and distinction, nor even the loss of that independence which is so vital to the commonweal . . . The last tragedy, and the saddest, is when the treasured language dies slowly out, when winter falls upon the legendary remembrance of a people . . . It is a strange thing: that a nation can hold within itself an ancient race, standing for the lost, beautiful, mysterious ancient world, can see it fading through its dim twilight, without heed to preserve that which might yet be preserved, without interest even in that which once gone cannot come again. The old Gaelic race is in its twilight indeed; but now, alas! it is the hastening twilight after the feast of Samhain, when winter is come at last, out of the hills, down the glens, on the four winds of the world.

FIONA MacLEOD, *The Winged Destiny*
(London: Heinemann 1910, pp.223-5)

THE LACK OF A WHOLE LANGUAGE

Scotsmen feel in one language and think in another . . . The curse of Scottish literature is the lack of a whole language, which finally means the lack of a whole mind.

EDWIN MUIR, *Scott and Scotland*
(London: Routledge 1936, pp.21-2)

A LINGUISTIC REFORMATION

In 1560 the Reformation took place in Scotland and the English Bible, translated in that same year by English refugees in Geneva, was, in default of a Scots translation which never existed, circulated throughout the land. Its language became familiar to the people as the language of solemnity and abstract thought, of theological and philosophical disputation, while Scots remained as the language of ordinary life, of the domestic, sentimental and comic, and from here we can trace the split mind that Scots have had about their native language ever since.

DAVID MURISON, *The Guid Scots Tongue*
(Edinburgh: 1977, p.5)

THE LOSS OF LANGUAGE

He who loses his language loses his world. The Highlander who loses his language loses his world.

IAIN CRICHTON SMITH, 'Shall Gaelic
Die?' (translated from his Gaelic original),
Selected Poems 1955-1980 (Edinburgh:
Macdonald 1981, p.135)

DORIC DIALECT

The people here [Edinburgh] are so social and attentive in their civilities to strangers, that I am insensibly sucked into the channel of their manners and customs, although they are in fact much more different from ours than you can imagine – That difference, however, which struck me very much at my first arrival, I now hardly perceive, and my ear is perfectly reconciled to the Scotch accent, which I find even agreeable in the mouth of a pretty woman – It is a sort of Doric dialect, which gives an idea of amiable simplicity.

TOBIAS SMOLLETT, *Humphry Clinker* (1771)

ON A COCK-HORSE

If the Doric is to come back alive, it will come first on a cock-horse.

WILLIAM SOUTAR, letter of 1931 to Hugh
MacDiarmid (in National Library of Scotland)

LALLAN

'What tongue does your auld bookie speak?'

He'll spier; an' I, his mou to steik: *ask, mouth, close*
'No bein' fit to write in Greek,
    I wrote in Lallan,
Dear to my heart as the peat reek,
    Auld as Tantallon.

'Few spak it then, an' noo there's nane.
My puir auld sangs like a' their lane,
Their sense, that aince was braw an' plain,
    Tint a'thegether,   *lost*
Like runes upon a standin' stane
    Amang the heather.'

ROBERT LOUIS STEVENSON (1850-94),
'The Maker to Posterity'

DIMINUTIVES

The Scottish language has one beauty, in which it greatly excels the English, and in which also it conforms to the Italian; that of diminutives, which are created at pleasure, and expressed in one word, by the addition of a letter or syllable; thus, they say 'man*ny*, dog*gy*, cat*ty*,' for a little man, dog, or cat; 'wife*y*,' for a little wife; and and if it was necessary to speak of an inanimate thing, they do it also in the same manner; as 'a buckle*y*, knife*y*, book*y*, house*y*,' for a little buckle, knife, book, and house. I need not tell you how emphatical this makes their tongue, and what an improvement it is on ours.

EDWARD TOPHAM, *Letters from Edinburgh*
(1776, Letter VII)

URQUHART'S UNIVERSAL LANGUAGE

All the languages in the world will be beholding to this, and this to none . . . The greatest wonder of all is, that of all the languages in the world, it is the easiest to learn; a boy of ten yeers old, being able to attaine to the knowledge thereof, in three moneths space; because there are in it many facilitations

for the memory, which no other language hath but itself . . .

SIR THOMAS URQUHART,
The Discoverie of a most Exquisite Jewel (1652)

9

LOVE AND LUST

A BED, A BED

'A bed, a bed', Clerk Saunders said,
  'And ay a bed for you and me';
'Never a ane', said the gay lady,
  'Till ance we twa married be.'

ANON, 'Clerk Saunders', in Francis James
Child, *The English and Scottish Popular Ballads*
(1882-98, 69B)

SAIL THE SEAS

I could sail the seas with my Jackie Faa,
  I could sail the seas with my dearie;
I could sail the seas with my Jackie Faa,
  And with pleasure could drown with my dearie.

ANON, 'The Gypsy Laddie', in Francis James
Child, *The English and Scottish Popular Ballads*
(1882-98, 200C)

ALL FOR YOUR CONVENIENCE

John Anderson, my jo, John,
  When first that ye began,
Ye had as good a tail-tree,
  As ony ither man;
But now it's waxen wan, John,
  And wrinkles to and fro;
I've twa gae-ups for ae gae-down,
  John Anderson, my jo.

I'm backit like a salmon,
　I'm breastit like a swan;
My wame it is a down-cod,
　My middle ye may span:
Frae my tap-knot to my tae, John,
　I'm like the new-fa'n snow;
And it's a' for your convenience,
　John Anderson, my jo.

ANON, in *The Merry Muses of Caledonia*
(*c.* 1800)

THE BALL OF KIRRIEMUIR

Did ye hear about the Ball, my lads?
The Ball of Kirriemuir?
Some came for the dancing
But they mostly came to whore.
　Sing balls to your partner,
　Arse against the wall;
　If you canna get fucked on a Saturday night
　Ye'll never get fucked at all!

ANON, 'The Ball of Kirriemuir'

FINE MEN

They [men] are something fine; and every woman is loath to
admit to herself that her husband is not one. When she
marries, even though she has been a very trivial person, there
is in her some vague stirring toward a worthy life, as well as a
fear of her capacity for evil. She knows her chance lies in him.
If there is something good in him, what is good in her finds it
and they join forces against the baser parts.

J.M. BARRIE, *The Twelve-Pound Look* (1910)

AN UNACCOUNTABLE ALARM

I this day began to feel an unaccountable alarm of unexpected evil: a little heat in the members of my body sacred to Cupid, very like a symptom of that distemper with which Venus, when cross, takes it into her head to plague her votaries. But then I had run no risks. I had been with no woman but Louisa; and sure she could not have such a thing. Away then with such idle fears, such groundless uneasy apprehensions!

JAMES BOSWELL, Journal (18 January 1763)

A MAD DESIRE

Unhappie is the man for evermair
That tills the sand and sawis in the air;
But twice unhappier is he, I lairn,
That feedis in his hairt a mad desire,
And follows on a woman throu the fire,
Led by a blin, and teachit by a bairn.

MARK ALEXANDER BOYD (1563-1601),
'Venus and Cupid'

THE TRUE PATHOS

But to conclude my silly rhyme
(I'm scant o' verse and scant o' time):
To make a happy fireside clime
    To weans and wife,   *children*
That's the true pathos and sublime
    Of human life.

ROBERT BURNS (1759-96),
'Epistle to Dr Blacklock'

HEY FOR HOUGHMAGANDIE

O gie the lass her fairin' lad,   *food*
  O gie the lass her fairin',
An' something else she'll gie to you,
    That's waly worth the wearin';   *well*
Syne coup her o'er amang the creels,   *overturn*

When ye hae taen your brandy,
The mair she bangs the less she squeels,
An' hey for houghmagandie.   *fornication*

ROBERT BURNS (1759-96),
'Gie the Lass her Fairin"

THE TREE OF LIFE

Oh, what a peacemaker is a guid weel-willy pintle! It is the
mediator, the guarantee, the umpire, the bond of union, the
solemn league and covenant, the plenipotentiary, the Aaron's
rod, the Jacob's staff, the prophet Elisha's pot of oil, the
Ahasuerus' sceptre, the horn of plenty, the Tree of Life
between Man and Woman.

ROBERT BURNS, letter of 3 March 1788
to Robert Ainslie

A LONG, LONG KISS

A long, long kiss, a kiss of youth, and love,
    And beauty, all concentrating like rays
Into one focus, kindled from above;
    Such kisses as belong to early days,
Where heart, and soul, and sense, in concert move,
    And the blood's lava, and the pulse a blaze,
Each kiss a heart-quake, – for a kiss's strength,
I think it must be reckoned by its length.

LORD BYRON, *Don Juan*
(1819-24, II, clxxxvi)

THE HEAD OF THE HOUSE

The Man should bear rule in the house and not the Woman. This is
an eternal axiom, the Law of Nature herself which no mortal
departs from unpunished. I have meditated on this many long
years, and every day it grows plainer to me; I must not and I
cannot live in a house of which I am not head. I should be

miserable myself, and make all about me miserable.

THOMAS CARLYLE, letter of 2 April 1826
to his future wife Jane Welsh

A WIFE'S COMPLAINT

Ay when that caribald carl wald climb on my wame,

dirty old man, belly

Then am I dangerus and dain and dour of my will;

disdainful, unyielding

Yet let I never that larbar my leggis gae between, *impotent man*
To fyl my flesh, na fumyll me, without a fee great; *grope*
And thoch his penie puirly me payis in bed, *penis*
His purse pays richly in recompense efter:
For, or he climb on my corse, that carybald forlane, *body, forlorn*
I have condition of a curch of kersp allther finest, *kerchief of gauze*
A goun of engranyt claith, richty gaily furrit, *scarlet cloth*
A ring with a royall stane, or other rich jewel,
Or rest of his rousty raid, thoch he were rede wod:

feeble ride, stark mad

For all the buddis of Johne Blunt, when he abone climis,

bribes, Stupid John

Me think the baid dear abocht, sae bawch are his werkis;

bribe, weak

And thus I sell him solace, thoch I it sour think;
Frae sic a syre, God you save, my sweet sisteris dear!

WILLIAM DUNBAR (*c.* 1460-*c.* 1520),
'The Tretis of the Twa Mariit Wemen and
the Wedo'

ELENA'S RED DRESS

I was a young girl and my present was a red dress. It was a
miracle, it fitted me. It was stunning and, wee balloon that I
was, I cried when I tried it on. I have never seen a thing so
fine, covered in red sequins like fish scales, a glittering slinky
fish, and suddenly I wasn't embarrassed about having breasts
anymore. Of course I was never allowed to wear it. Good

girls didn't wear red, red was a putana's colour, red was what whore's wore.

> MARCELLA EVARISTI, *Commedia*
> (Edinburgh: Salamander Press 1983, p.26)

THE RULING POWER

Thus, from less to more, our argobargoling was put an end to; and from that time I was the ruling power in our domicile, which has made it the habitation of quiet ever since; for from that moment I never laid down the rod of authority, which I achieved with such a womanly sleight of hand.

> JOHN GALT, 'The Gudewife' (1833; rept.
> in ed. Douglas Gifford, *Scottish Short Stories*
> *1800-1900*, London: Calder and Boyars 1971,
> p.69)

A WOMAN

She was beautiful. That word must suffice. Her dresses were short, allowing me (and others, oh lucky breed) to see her lovely knees and thighs above . . . She was purity and maturity, lust and love. A woman. My woman. And the stalk grew, for the first time. Mine, really mine. I loved her. We loved each other.

> GILES GORDON, *About a Marriage*
> (1972; rept. Harmondsworth: Penguin Books
> 1974, pp.69-70)

THE GREATEST SNARE

In particular, I brought myself to despise, if not to abhor, the beauty of women, looking on it as the greatest snare to which mankind are subjected, and though young men and maidens, and even old women, (my mother among the rest,) taxed me with being an unnatural wretch, I gloried in my acquisition; and to this day, am thankful for having escaped the most dangerous of all snares.

> JAMES HOGG, *The Private Memoirs and*
> *Confessions of a Justified Sinner* (1824)

EQUAL PARTNERSHIP

The tender sentiments and affections which engage the parties into this relation of marriage, plainly declare it to be a state of equal partnership or friendship, and not such a one wherein the one party stipulates to himself a right of governing in all domestic affairs, and the other promises subjection.

> FRANCIS HUTCHESON,
> *A System of Moral Philosophy* (1755)

A WOMANLY WOMAN

I like a womanly woman. Nane o' your walking-sticks for Harry Lauder!

> SIR HARRY LAUDER, *Ticklin' Talks*
> (Dundee: D.C. Thomson n.d., p.239)

LADY SENSUALITY SPEAKS

Lovers awake! Behold the fiery sphere,
Behold the natural daughter of Venus!
Behold, lovers, this lusty lady clear,
The fresh fountain of knightës amorous,
Replete with joys, douce and delicious.
Or who would make to Venus observance
In my mirthful chamber melodious?
There shall they find all pastime and pleasance.
Behold my head, behold my gay attire,
Behold my neck, lovesome and lily-white;
Behold my visage flaming as the fire,
Behold my paps, of portraiture perfite!
To look on me lovers have great delight

> SIR DAVID LINDSAY (*c.* 1490-1555), in
> Robert Kemp's acting version of *The Satire of
> the Three Estates* (London: Heinemann 1951,
> p.6)

A GLIMPSE

A lovely woman taking off her clothing's

delight to men: a glimpse of promised seas
to carry freights of bliss and soft supposings,
meeting the distance of a moment's ease.

MAURICE LINDSAY, *A Net to Catch the Winds*
(London: Robert Hale 1981, p.37)

A COLD BATH

Like many Scots, I was physically a slow developer . . . For
most of us at public schools, sex education in the early thirties
was mainly a matter of lavatorial whisperings. On my
fourteenth birthday my father presented me with a curious
book called something like *What Every Boy Should Know*. The
gist of its message was that if I felt the weakness of the sexual
drive overcoming me, I must pray to God for protection and
take violent exercise, followed by a cold bath. If I indulged in
shameful self-gratification, God would be affronted and the
future efficacy of my member permanently impaired.

MAURICE LINDSAY, *Thank You For Having
Me* (London: Robert Hale 1983, pp.26-7)

MEN'S DREAMS

I'll be a torment, haunt men's dreams,
I'll wear my stockings black with seams.

I'll rouge my cleavage, flaunt myself, my heels
will be perilously high, oh
but I won't sway.

LIZ LOCHHEAD, 'Bawd', *The Grimm Sisters*
(London: Next Editions 1981, p.18)

THE BRIDE

O wha's the bride that cairries the bunch
O' thistles blinterin' white?   *gleaming*
Her cuckold bridegroom little dreids
What he sall ken this nicht.

For closer than gudeman can come
And closer to'r than herself',
Wha didna need her maidenheid
Has wrocht his purpose fell.

HUGH MacDIARMID, 'A Drunk Man Looks
at the Thistle', *Complete Poems 1920-76*, eds.
W.R. Aitken and Michael Grieve (London:
Martin Brian and O'Keeffe 1978, p.102).

MILLIONS OF CHILDREN

Millions o' wimmen bring forth in pain
Millions o' bairns that are no' worth ha'en'.

Wull ever a wumman be big again
Wi's muckle's a Christ? Yech, there's nae sayin'.

HUGH MacDIARMID, 'A Drunk Man Looks
at the Thistle', *Complete Poems*, (*ibid*, p.103)

THE GREAT DISCOVERY

'The Colonel's too gallant, too romantic, too old',
She sadly admitted, "it's true
To appreciate the Great Discovery of the Age
– That women like It too!'

HUGH MacDIARMID, 'Ode to All Rebels',
Complete Poems, (*ibid*, p.491)

FEMALE ACCOMPLISHMENTS

When men begin to disuse their ancient barbarous practices, when their attention is not wholly engrossed by the pursuit of military reputation, when they have made some progress in arts, and have attained to a proportional degree of refinement, they are necessarily led to set a value upon those female accomplishments and virtues which have so much influence upon every species of improvement, and which contribute in so many different ways to multiply the comforts of life.

JOHN MILLAR, *The Origin of the Distinction
of Ranks* (1779 edtn)

WILD CIRCUIT

Woman is
acute angles of feeling;
wires exposed to the world,
connected at the womb.

Wild circuit –
sending charges through
the reasoned running of mankind,
which seizes up and shocks.

TESSA RANSFORD, 'Woman',
Light of the Mind (Edinburgh: Ramsay Head
Press 1980, p.38)

A FERVENT FIRE

Luve is ane fervent fire,
Kendillit without desire;
Short pleisure, lang displeisure,
Repentence is the hire;
Ane puir treisure without meisure:
Luve is ane fervent fire.

ALEXANDER SCOTT (*c.* 1515-83),
'A Rondel of Luve'

UNREQUITED LOVE

Whatten ane glaiket fule am I,   *idiotic*
To slay myself with melancholy,
    Sen weill I ken I may nocht get her!
Or what sould be the cause, and why,
    To break my hairt, and nocht the better?

My hairt, sen thou may nocht her please,
Adieu, as gude luve cumis as gaes;
    Go choose ane uther and forget her.
God give him dolour and disease
    That breakis his hairt, and nocht the better.

ALEXANDER SCOTT (*c.* 1515-83),
'To Luve Unluvit'

A BONNIE COU

    – Ah, she was a bonnie cou!   *cow*
Saxteen, maybe sevinteen, nae mair,
Her mither in attendance, *comme il faut*
Pour les jeunes filles bien élevées,
    Drinkan like a bluidie whaul tae!
Wee paps, round and ticht and fou
Like sweet Pomona in the oranger grove;
Her shanks were lang, but no ower lang, and plump,
    A lassie's shanks,
Wi the meisurance o Venus –
    Achteen inch the hoch frae heuchle-bane til knap
                                   thigh, hip-bone, knee
    Achteen inch the cauf frae knap til cuit   *ankle*
As is the true perfectioun calculate
By the Auntients efter due regaird
For this and that,
      The true meisurance
O' the Venus dei Medici,
    The Aphrodite Analyomene
And aa the goddeses o hie antiquitie –
    Siclike were the shanks and hochs
O' Sandra the cou o' the auld Black Bull.

                        SYDNEY GOODSIR SMITH, *Under the*
                        Eildon Tree (Edinburgh: Serif Books 1948,
                        revd. 1954, 'Elegy XIII)

THE TRYST

    O luely, luely, cam she in
    And luely she lay doun:
    I kent her be her caller lips   *fresh*
    And her breists sae sma' and roun'.

          WILLIAM SOUTAR (1898-1943), 'The Tryst'

MEN AND WOMEN

[O]f the misbeggoten changelings who call themselves men,

and prate intolerably over dinner-table, I never saw one who seemed worthy to inspire love . . . About women I entertain a somewhat different opinion; but there, I have the misfortune to be a man.

ROBERT LOUIS STEVENSON, *Virginibus Puerisque* (1881, 'On Falling in Love')

A YOUNG FAIR LADY

Alone she sat, and pensive as may be
   A young fair lady, wishful of a mate;
Yet with her teeth held now and then a-picking,
Her stomach to refresh, the breast-bone of a chicken.

WILLIAM TENNANT, *Anster Fair* (1812, I, 13)

FOR A WOMAN

Meldrum was speaking again, raising his voice this time, and it wasn't exactly the language of an army deserter. 'Men have waded through blood and braved fire and water for a woman like yourself, quine; fought and died for them – songs and poetry and great ballads have been written about it, and mony times they didna get their woman, for they were crossed by fate. But Audie gets a woman like you just 'cause he's a dreep. A' he has to do is stand and look miserable at a street corner and one of Heaven's finest angels is sent down to comfort him.'

DAVID TOULMIN, *Blown Seed* (1976; rept. London: Pan Books 1978, p.164)

LECHER

But hearken, good fellows, the spigot ill betake you, and whirl round your brains, if you do not give ear! This little lecher [Gargantua] was always groping his nurses and governesses, upside down, arsiversy, topsiturvy, harri bourriquet, with a Yacco haick, kyck gio! handling them very rudely in jumbling and tumbling them to keep them going; for he had already begun to exercise the tools and put his codpiece in practice. Which codpiece, or *braguette*, his governesses did every day deck up and adorn with fair nosegays, curious rubies, sweet flowers and fine silken tufts, and very pleasantly would pass their time in taking you know what between their fingers, and dandling it, till it did revive and creep up to the bulk and stiffness of a suppository, or street magdaleon, which is a hard rolled up salve spread upon leather. Then did they burst out in laughing, when they saw it lift up its ears, as if the sport had liked them. One of them would call it her pillicock, her fiddle-diddle, her staff of love, her tickle-gizzard, her gentle-titler. Another, her sugarplum, her kingo, her old rowley, her touch-trap, her flap dowdle. Another again, her branch of coral, her placket-racket, her Cyprian sceptre, her tibit, her bob-lady. And some of the other women would give these names, my Roger, my cockatoo, my nimble-wimble, bush-beater, claw-buttock, eavesdropper, pick-lock, pioneer, bully-ruffin, smell-smock, trouble-gusset, my lusty live sausage, my crimson chitterlin, rump-splitter, shove-devil, down right to it, stiff and stout, in and to, at her again, my coney-burrow-ferret, wily-beguiley, my pretty rogue.

SIR THOMAS URQUHART (*c.* 1611-60),
translation of Rabelais, *Gargantua*
and Pantagruel (1532, Book I, Ch. 11)

10

NATIONAL INSTITUTIONS

THE LOCH NESS MYSTERY

The great appeal of the Loch Ness mystery is perhaps the way in which it offers everyone the chance to become an amateur sleuth, pore over the evidence, visit the dark mysterious waters, and concoct a new theory about what it is which has baffled the world for so long . . . After fifty years one conclusion about the mystery can reasonably be drawn. There is no scientific evidence whatsoever of monsters in Loch Ness, and a handful of individuals will go on seeing them there.

> RONALD BINNS, *The Loch Ness Mystery Solved* (1983; rept. London: W.H. Allen 1984, p.220)

A BLACK AFFRONT

– As for the Kirk I shall not speak of it!
Intolerable abuse of God and time
and word, insult to all creation's many-
bodied and marvellous perceptions, it was
a black affront to infancy's receptiveness.

> DAVID BLACK (born 1941),
> 'Parsifal Part One'

SIR WALTER SCOTT

Scott was a master but not a schoolmaster of language, and sometimes grammar and syntax go by the board.

> JOHN BUCHAN, *Sir Walter Scott*
> (London: Cassell 1932, p.337)

ROUND THE INGLE

The chearfu' supper done, wi' serious face,
   They, round the ingle, form a circle wide;
The sire turns o'er, wi' patriarchal grace,
   The big ha'-Bible, ance his father's pride.
   His bonnet rev'rently is laid aside,
His lyart haffets wearing thin and bare;   *grey sidelocks*
   Those strains that once did sweet in Zion glide,
He wales a portion with judicious care,   *selects*
And 'Let us worship God!' he says, with solemn air.

> ROBERT BURNS (1759-96),
> 'The Cotter's Saturday Night'

A GLORIOUS FEAST

A fig for those by law protected!
Liberty's a glorious feast,
Courts for cowards were erected,
Churches built to please the priest!

> ROBERT BURNS (1759-96),
> 'Love and Liberty'

NATURE'S FIRE

A set o' dull, conceited hashes   *dunderheads*
Confuse their brains in college-classes,
They gang in stirks, and come out asses,   *young bullocks*
     Plain truth to speak;
An' syne they think to climb Parnassus   *then*
     By dint o' Greek!

Gie me ae spark o' Nature's fire,
That's a' the learning I desire;
Then, tho' I drudge thro' dub an' mire   *puddle*
     At pleugh or cart,
My Muse, tho' hamely in attire,
     May touch the heart.

> ROBERT BURNS (1759-96),
> 'Epistle to J. Lapraik'

THE TRUE UNIVERSITY

The true University of these days is a Collection of Books.

THOMAS CARLYLE, *On Heroes,*
Hero-Worship, and the Heroic in History (1841,
'The Hero as Man of Letters')

THE STERN DOCTRINES OF CALVINISM

I well remember that the stern doctrines of Calvinism lay as a terrible nightmare upon me . . . I grew up treasuring within me the fact that my father had risen and left the Presbyterian Church [in Dunfermline] one day when the minister preached the doctrine of infant damnation. This was shortly after I had made my first appearance.

ANDREW CARNEGIE, *Autobiography*
(London: Constable 1920, pp.22-3)

THE LION TAMED

In the beginning, there were these ambitious plans for promoting a spectacular educational programme for Scotland, for building up a new learned class of specialists around the Universities, and for consolidating Edinburgh's historic role as the cultural capital of an education-minded country; but, in the end, after it was made clear that there was to be no financial aid for these schemes, the proposed advance became a deliberate retreat; the thistle motif gave way to that of the mountain daisy, and the rampant lion turned into a wee, sleekit, cowering, timorous beastie.

G.E. DAVIE, *The Democratic Intellect*
(Edinburgh: Edinburgh University Press 1961,
pp.72-3)

BEFORE AND AFTER

Before the Reformation, colour and music and splendid robes were part of the law of Scotland and Scottish court and church

. . . until very recent times, the ministers of the Church of Scotland wore black and colour was not to be seen in the kirks. Music was absent, except for the stilted chant of the metrical psalms, and drink was, of course, a demon of the Devil.

NICHOLAS FAIRBAIRN, *The Scotsman*,
24 May 1984, p.11

THE SEEDS OF EVERY FORM

No constitution is formed by concert, no government is copied from a plan. The members of a small state contend for equality; the members of a greater, find themselves classed in a certain manner that lays a foundation for monarchy. They proceed from one form of government to another, by easy transitions, and frequently under old names adopt a new constitution. The seeds of every form are lodged in human nature; they spring up and ripen with the season. The prevalence of a particular species is often derived from an imperceptible ingredient mingled in the soil.

ADAM FERGUSON, *Essay on the History of
Civil Society* (1768 edtn)

EDUCATION AND ACTION

Education is not merely by and for the sake of thought, it is in a still higher degree by and for the sake of action. Just as the man of science must think and experiment alternately, so too must artist, author and scholar alternate creation or study with participation in the life around them. For it is only by thinking things out as one lives them, and living things out as one thinks them, that a man or a society can really be said to think or even live at all.

PATRICK GEDDES, Lecture of 1895, quoted
in Philip Boardman, *The Worlds of Patrick
Geddes* (London: Routledge and Kegan Paul
1978, p.130)

THE STOOL OF REPENTANCE

At certain periods and in certain districts there must nearly always have been someone on the stool of repentance. This could happen without any incredible amount of immorality in the parish, for a case of adultery for which complete satisfaction was offered might involve 26 appearances of each of the guilty parties, and for lesser offences six or three appearances of each would be usual, the man and woman being generally – though not everywhere – pilloried at different services.

G.D. HENDERSON, *The Scottish Ruling Elder*
(London: James Clarke 1935, p.116)

THE SPLIT MIND

O Knox he was a bad man
he split the Scottish mind.
the one half he made cruel
and the other half unkind.

ALAN JACKSON (b. 1938), 'Knox (2)'

FLATTER NO FLESH

'Without the preiching Place, Madam [= Mary Queen of Scots], I think few have Occasioun to be offendit at me; and thare, Madam, I am not Master of myself, bot man obey him quho comands me to speik plane, and to flater no Flesch upon the Face of the Eirth.'

JOHN KNOX, *Historie of the Reformatioun in Scotland* (1586; the Matthew Crawfurd text of 1732)

DEPRESSION

No one intended, when they told a little boy when and how to clean his teeth, and that his teeth would fall out if he was bad, together with Presbyterian Sunday School and all the rest of it, to produce forty-five years later the picture of a typical obsessive involutional depression. This syndrome is one of the specialities of Scotland.

R.D. LAING, *The Politics of the Family* (1971; rept. Harmondsworth: Penguin Books 1976, p.98)

ONE OF US

heh jimmy
ma right insane yirra pape
ma right insane yirwanny us jimmy
see it nyir eyes
wanny uz

TOM LEONARD, 'The Good Thief',
Intimate Voices (Newcastle: Galloping Dog
Press 1984, p.9)

JOHN THE COMMON-WEAL ON THE LAW

A petty picking thief is hanged,
But he that all the world has wronged –
A cruel tyrant, a strong transgressor,
A common public plain oppressor –
By bribes may he obtain favours
Of treasures and compositors,
And through laws, consistorial,
Prolix, corrupt and perpetual,
The common people are so put under,
Though they be poor, it is no wonder!

SIR DAVID LINDSAY (c. 1490–1555), in
Robert Kemp's acting version of *The Satire of
the Three Estates* (London: Heinemann 1951,
pp.49-50)

BEYOND PAROCHIALISM

The Scotch now no longer consider it as a matter of perfect

certainty, that the Pope is the Anti-christ, and the Church of Rome the Babylon of the Revelations. They do full honour to those heroic and holy spirits who wrought the great work of the Reformation, but they do not doubt that even those who nominally adhere to the ancient faith, have derived great benefit from the establishment of the new. They refuse to consider the kingdom of Christ as composed only of the little province which they themselves inhabit.

JOHN GIBSON LOCKHART, *Peter's Letters to his Kinsfolk* (1819, Letter LXXIII)

THE REFORMATION

What the Reformation did was to snuff out what must otherwise have developed into the most brilliant national culture in history.

FIONN MacCOLLA, *At the Sign of the Clenched Fist* (Edinburgh: Macdonald 1967, p.204)

BURNS SUPPERS

No' wan in fifty kens a wurd Burns wrote
But misapplied is a'body's property,
And gin there was his like alive the day   *if*
They'd be the last a kennin' haund to gi'e –

Croose London Scotties wi' their braw shirt fronts   *conceited*
And a' their fancy freen's, rejoicin'   *friends*
That similah gatherings in Timbuctoo,
Bagdad – and Hell, nae doot – are voicin'

Burns' sentiments o' universal love,
In pidgin English or in wild-fowl Scots,
And toastin' ane wha's nocht to them but an
Excuse for faitherin' Genius wi' *their* thochts.

HUGH MacDIARMID, 'A Drunk Man Looks at the Thistle', *Complete Poems,* eds. W.R. Aitken and Michael Grieve (London: Martin Brian and O'Keeffe 1978, p.84)

GREATER TRUTHS

There are greater truths than can be written on the blackboard.

KEN MORRICE, 'Love School', *Relations*
(Aberdeen: Rainbow Books 1979, p.25)

THE AULD KIRK

The gude auld Kirk o' Scotland,
    The wild winds round her blaw,
And when her foemen hear her sough,
    They prophecy her fa';
But what although her fate has been
    Amang the floods to sit –
The gude auld Kirk o' Scotland,
    She's nae in ruins yet!

GEORGE MURRAY (1819-68),
'The Auld Kirk o' Scotland'

THE TAWSE

I taught in a system that depended on the *tawse*, as we called the belt in Scotland. My father used it and I followed suit, without ever thinking about the rights and wrongs of it – until the day when I myself, as a headmaster, belted a boy for insolence. A new, sudden thought came to me. What am I doing? This boy is small, and I am big. Why am I hitting someone not my own size? I put my tawse in the fire and never hit a child again.

A.S. NEILL, *Neill! Neill! Orange Peel!*
(1973; rept. London: Quartet Books 1977,
p.21)

THE KIRK

Getting ready for the kirk [in Forfar] was hateful to us. We struggled with clumsy cufflinks: we resentfully stood to have

olive oil rubbed into our hair. We were all dressed up with
nowhere to go – nowhere, at any rate, that we wanted to go.
We knew there lay before us an hour and a half of extreme
boredom, of sitting on a hard pew with upright back – only
the rich had cushions – of listening to dull psalms and hymns
and a seemingly interminable sermon by Dr Caie.

A.S. NEILL, *Neill! Neill! Orange Peel!*
(*Ibid*, p.11)

A BRIEF EDUCATION

I was born near four miles from Nith-head,
Where fourteen years I got my bread;
My learning it can soon be told,
Ten weeks when I was seven years old.

ISABEL PAGAN (1741-1821),
'Account of the Author's Lifetime'

THE TARTAN PLAID

The Plaid itself gives pleasure to the sight,
To see how all its sets imbibe the light;
Forming some way, which even to me lies hid,
White, black, blue, yellow, purple, green, and red.
Let Newton's royal club thro' prisms stare,
To view celestial dyes with curious care,
I'll please myself, nor shall my sight ask aid
Of crystal gimcracks to survey the plaid.

ALLAN RAMSAY (1686-1758), 'Tartana'

NOT PROVEN

[T]he jury gave that bastard verdict, *Not proven*. I hate that
Caledonian *medium quid*. One who is not *proven guilty* is
innocent in the eye of law.

SIR WALTER SCOTT, *Journal*
19 February 1827

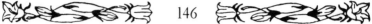

A REFORMED STATE

In some countries, as in Scotland, where the government was weak, unpopular, and not very firmly established, the Reformation was strong enough to overturn, not only the church, but the state likewise for attempting to support the church.

ADAM SMITH, *The Wealth of Nations*
(1784 edtn, Bk. V, Ch. i)

THE AUTHORITY OF A CHIEFTAIN

We come now to explain how one man came to have more authority than the rest, and how chieftains were introduced. A nation consists of many families who have met together, and agreed to live with one another. At their public meetings there will always be one of superior influence to the rest, who will in a great measure direct and govern their resolutions, which is all the authority of a chieftain in a barbarous country.

ADAM SMITH, *Lectures on Justice, Police,
Revenue and Arms* (1896)

MISS JEAN BRODIE ON TEACHING

'Give me a girl at an impressionable age, and she is mine for life.'

MURIEL SPARK, *The Prime of Miss Jean Brodie*
(1961; rept. Penguin Books 1965, p.9)

11

PLACES

ABERDEEN

The sea-gray toun, the stane-gray sea,
The cushat's croudle mells wi the sea-maw's skirl
                                      pigeon's coo, mingles
Whaur baith gae skaichan fish-guts doun the quays
                                           scavenging
Or scrannan crumbs in cracks o the thrang causeys,
                                         scraping, busy
A lichthous plays the lamp-post owre a close,
The traffic clappers through a fisher's clachan
                                             village
Whaur aa the vennels spulyie names frae the sea,
                                      alleys, plunder
And kirks and crans clanjamfrie,
Heaven and haven mixter-maxtered heave
                                          confused
To the sweel o the same saut tide.

                     ALEXANDER SCOTT (born 1920),
                     'Heart of Stone'

ANSTRUTHER

And, from our steeple's pinnacle outspread,
    The town's long colours flare and flap on high,
Whose anchor, blazon'd fair in green and red,
    Curls, pliant to each breeze that whistles by:
Whilst, on the boltsprit, stern, and topmast-head,
    Of brig and sloop that in the harbour lie,
Streams the red gaudery of flags in air,
All to salute the morn of ANSTER FAIR.

                     WILLIAM TENNANT, *Anster Fair*
                     (1812, Canto III, vii)

ARBUTHNOTT

Neither Lowland nor Highland, it is a place without history,

though the national hero of Scotland, Sir William Wallace . . .
is supposed to have hidden in a yew-tree near the present
manse during the early days of the rebellion against the
southern aliens.

> JAMES LESLIE MITCHELL, *The Thirteenth
> Disciple* (1931; rept. Edinburgh: Paul Harris
> 1981, p.15)

BUCHAN FARMS

Conditions on some of the farms [of Buchan] were as menial
and sordid as they were for the slaves in the American Deep
South; in some cases even worse, barring the use of the whip,
with food at the barest minimum of existence, and sanitation
non-existent. Sometimes there was an intimacy between the
slave families and their masters which was seldom reached
among Scottish farm workers and their employers.

> DAVID TOULMIN, *A Chiel Among Them*
> (Aberdeen: Gourdas House 1982, p.85)

CLYDE

And call they this Improvement? – to have changed,
My native Clyde, thy once romantic shore,
Where Nature's face is banished and estranged,
And Heaven reflected in thy wave no more;
Whose banks, that sweetened May-day's breath before,
Lie sere and leafless now in summer's beam,
With sooty exhalations covered o'er;
And for the daisied green sward, down thy stream
Unsightly brick-lanes smoke, and clanking engines gleam.

> THOMAS CAMPBELL (1777-1844),
> 'Lines on Revisiting a Scottish River'

CULLODEN, A VISION

Oh! Drumossie, thy bleak moor shall, ere many generations

have passed away, be stained with the best blood of the Highlands. Glad am I that I will not see that day, for it will be a fearful period; heads will be lopped off by the score, and no mercy will be shown or quarter given on either side.

KENNETH MacKENZIE (17th century), the Brahan Seer, quoted in Alexander Mackenzie, *The Prophecies of the Brahan Seer* (1899; rept. Golspie: Sutherland Press 1970, p.47)

CULLODEN

Mourn, hapless Caledonia, mourn
Thy banish'd peace, thy laurels torn!
Thy sons, for valour long renown'd,
Lie slaughter'd on their native ground;
Thy hospitable roofs no more
Invite the stranger to the door;
In smoky ruins sunk they lie,
The monuments of cruelty.

TOBIAS SMOLLETT (1721-71), 'The Tears of Scotland'

DUNBEATH

Sea-fishing and crofting were the only two occupations of the people [of Dunbeath], and however the rewards of their labour varied season to season, they were never greatly dissimilar over a whole year or over ten years. Thus in the course of centuries there had developed a communal feeling so genuine that the folk themselves never thought about it. They rejoiced and quarrelled, loved and fought, on a basis of social equality.

NEIL M. GUNN, *Highland River* (1937; rept. London: Arrow Books 1960, p.24)

DUNDEE A SINK OF ATROCITY

Dundee, certainly now, and for many years past, the most

blackguard place in Scotland . . . a sink of atrocity, which no moral flushing seems capable of cleansing. A Dundee criminal, especially if a lady, may be known, without any evidence about character, by the intensity of the crime, the audacious bar air, and the parting curses.

LORD COCKBURN, *Circuit Journeys* (1888; rept. Hawick: Byway Books 1983, p.239)

EDINBURGH'S SMELL

On stair, wi' tub or pat in hand,
The barefoot housemaids lo'e to stand,
That antrin fouk may ken how snell   *different, sharp*
Auld Reekie will at mornin' smell:
Then, wi' an inundation big as
The burn that 'neath the Nor' Loch brig is,
They kindly shower Edina's roses,
To quicken an' regale our noses.
Now some for this, wi' satire's leesh,
Hae gi'en auld Edinbrough a creesh: *grease*
But without sourin nought is sweet;
The mornin' smells that hail our street
Prepare an' gently lead the way
To Simmer canty, braw, an' gay.   *summer*

ROBERT FERGUSSON, 'Auld Reekie' (1773)

EDINBURGH AND HEALTH

The violent gusts of wind, continually to be felt in the streets of Edinburgh are, I imagine, owing to its situation, and must be the cause of health to its inhabitants (they are very healthy); for had not the atmosphere of that city some powerful refiner, such as a constant high wind, it would, by its nauseous scents, poison the race of beings living in it.

SARAH MURRAY, *The Beauties of Scotland* (1799; rept. Hawick: Byway Books 1982, p.20)

EDINBURGH, SALISBURY CRAGS

If I were to choose a spot from which the rising or setting sun could be seen to the greatest possible advantage, it would be that wild path winding around the foot of the high belt of semi-circular rocks, called Salisbury Crags, and marking the verge of the steep descent which slopes down into the glen on the south-eastern side of the city of Edinburgh.

SIR WALTER SCOTT,
The Heart of Midlothian (1818, Ch. VIII)

EDINBURGH'S SMOKE

Well may Edinburgh be called Auld Reekie! And the houses stand so one above another, that none of the smoke wastes itself upon the desert air before the inhabitants have derived all the advantages of its odour and its smuts. You might smoke bacon by hanging it out of the window.

ROBERT SOUTHEY, *Journal of a Tour in Scotland in 1819* (London: John Murray 1929, p.13)

EDINBURGH

Edina, high in heaven wan,
Towered, templed, Metropolitan,
    Waited upon by hills,
River, and wide-spread ocean-tinged
By April light, or draped and fringed
    As April vapour wills.
Thou hangest, like a Cyclops' dream,
High in the shifting weather-gleam.

ALEXANDER SMITH, 'Edinburgh'
(*Last Leaves*, 1868)

EDINBURGH, GOOD IN PARTS

I wish you were in Edinboro' with me – it is quite lovely – bits of it.

OSCAR WILDE, letter of 17 December 1884
to E.W. Godwin

EDINBURGH, PRECIPITOUS CITY

I saw rain falling and the rainbow drawn
On Lammermuir. Hearkening I heard again
In my precipitous city beaten bells
Winnow the keen sea wind.

ROBERT LOUIS STEVENSON, 'To My
Wife', dedication of *Weir of Hermiston* (1896)

EDINBURGH'S GRANTON

Doun by the water there
Whar the black ships berth
Is a dernit life beneath –   *hidden*
Cauldbluid mortalities
Umercifu and ceaseless,
Thouchtless as the seasons' round,
As daith, as memories.

SYDNEY GOODSIR SMITH (1915-75),
'Granton'

EDINBURGH'S ROYAL MILE

From Holyroodhouse to the Castle the ridge runs, hard and high, like the rough spine of Edinburgh, and the tall houses are its vertebrae, and in its marrow is a wilder life than that which animates the dignified terraces and sedate Georgian houses below. Those lofty houses are not an aristocracy decayed and subdued, but an aristocracy debauched and ruined, sprawling in rags and dirt where once it flaunted itself in threadbare finery and three-piled pride, and lived in the high perfume of insolence and treachery and blood.

ERIC LINKLATER, *Magnus Merriman* (1934;
rept. Edinburgh: Macdonald 1982, pp.55-6)

EDINBURGH, PRINCES STREET

And [Edinburgh's] Princes Street with its split personality: on the northern side plate-glass windows offering gowns and green-grocery, settees and shortbread, books and bales of cloth; and a historic, jagged skyline flanking its southern side with smoke puffing up from the trough of the gardens against the black silhouette of the castle and rock.

JOAN LINGARD, *The Prevailing Wind* (1964; rept. Edinburgh: Paul Harris 1978, p.47)

EDINBURGH AND CALVINISM

All she was conscious of now was that some quality of life peculiar to Edinburgh and nowhere else had been going on unbeknown to her all the time, and however undesirable it might be, she felt deprived of it; however undesirable, she desired to know what it was, and to cease to be protected from it by enlightened people.

In fact, it was the religion of Calvin of which Sandy [Stranger] felt deprived, or rather a specified recognition of it.

MURIEL SPARK, *The Prime of Miss Jean Brodie* (1961; rept. Penguin Books 1965, p.108)

EDINBURGH'S MURKY LEITH

Hostile High Street gave the sign.
Holyrood made unmerciful
These eyes that saw the saturnine

Watchmen of murky Leith begin
To pump amiss the never-full
Heart of Midlothian, never mine.

MURIEL SPARK, 'Edinburgh Villanelle', *Going Up to Sotheby's* (St Albans: Granada Publishing 1982, p.80)

EDINBURGH, PRINCES STREET

Princes Street, Edinburgh, even in the most rushed of rush hours, you will be

a glade in a wood, I'll wrap myself
in your cool rusticity, I'll
foretell the weather, I'll be
a hick in the sticks.

NORMAN MacCAIG, 'Last Night in
New York', *Old Maps and New* (London:
The Hogarth Press 1978, p.97)

EDINBURGH, WAVERLEY STATION

Such multitudinous intercourse takes place
in Waverley station that I almost think
the city spreads from there, fertile, horripilating
in streets and terraces.

DAVID BLACK (born 1941),
'Parsifal Part One'

GLASGOW STREETS

City! I am true son of thine;
Ne'er dwelt I where great mornings shine
    Around the bleating pens;
Ne'er by the rivulets I strayed,
And ne'er upon my childhood weighed
    The silence of the glens.
Instead of shores where ocean beats,
I hear the ebb and flow of streets.

ALEXANDER SMITH, 'Glasgow'
(*City Poems*, 1857)

GLASGOW BELONGS TO ME

I belong to Glasgow
Dear Old Glasgow town!
But what's the matter with Glasgow?
For it's going round and round.
I'm only a common old working chap,
As anyone here can see,

But when I get a couple of drinks on a Saturday,
Glasgow belongs to me.

> WILL FYFFE (1885-1947),
> 'I Belong to Glasgow'

GLASGOW, DEPLORABLE CITY

Glasgow – that strange, deplorable city which has neither
sweetness nor pride, the vomit of a cataleptic commercialism
. . .

> JAMES LESLIE MITCHELL, *The Thirteenth
> Disciple* (1931; rept. Edinburgh: Paul Harris
> 1981, pp.68-9)

GLASGOW TENEMENTS

The misty smoke and the tenements of Glasgow, caught in
the light, made a magic of their own.

> GUY McCRONE, *The Philistines*
> (1947; rept. London: Pan Books 1978, p.28)

GLASGOW SLUMS

I walked to and from my work each day through a slum, for
there was no way of getting from the south side of Glasgow
to the city except through slums. These journeys filled me
with a sense of degradation: the crumbling houses, the twisted
faces, the obscene words casually heard in passing, the
ancient, haunting stench of pollution and decay, the arrogant
women, the mean men, the terrible children, daunted me, and
at last filled me with an immense, blind dejection.

> EDWIN MUIR, *An Autobiography*
> (London: The Hogarth Press 1954, pp.91-2)

GLASGOW

The houses are Glasgow, not the people – these

Are simply the food the houses live and grow on
Endlessly, drawing from their vulgarity
And pettiness and darkness of spirit
– Gorgonising the mindless generations,
Turning them all into filthy property,
Apt as the Karaunas by diabolic arts
To produce darkness and obscure the light of day.
To see or hear a clock in Glasgow's horrible,
Like seeing a dead man's watch, still going though he's dead.
Everything is dead except stupidity here.

> HUGH MacDIARMID, 'Glasgow',
> *Complete Poems*, eds. W.R. Aitken and Michael
> Grieve (London: Martin Brian and O'Keeffe
> 1978, p.1049)

GLASGOW, THE DEAR GREEN PLACE

Gles Chu! Glasgow! The dear green place! Now a vehicular
sclerosis, a congestion of activity! . . . A Calvinist, Protestant
city. The influx of Roman Catholic Irish and Continental Jews
had done nothing to change it, even if they had given to its
slum quarters an air of spurious romance. Even they in the
end became Calvinist. A city whose talents were all outward
and acquisitive. Its huge mad Victorian megalomaniacal art
gallery full of acquired art, its literature dumb or in exile, its
poetry a dull struggle in obscurity, its night life non-existent,
its theatres unsupported, its Sundays sabbatarian, its secular
life moderate and dull on the one hand and sordid, furtive and
predatory on the other.

> ARCHIE HIND, *The Dear Green Place*
> (London: Hutchinson 1966, pp.63-5)

GLASGOW AFTER THE BOMB

But the great thing about the way Glasgow is now is that if
there's a nuclear attack it'll look exactly the same afterwards.

> BILLY CONNOLLY, *Gullible's Travels*
> (London: Pavilion 1982, p.140)

GLASGOW'S REPUTATION

Glasgow now means nothing to the rest of Britain but unemployment, drunkenness and out-of-date radical militancy.

ALASDAIR GRAY, *1982 Janine*
(London: Jonathan Cape 1984, p.136)

GLENCOE, THE MASSACRE

You are hereby ordered to fall upon the Rebells, the McDonalds of Glenco, and putt all to the sword under seventy, you are to have a speciall care that the old fox and his sones doe upon no account escape your hands.

The official order for the Massacre of Glencoe,
signed by Major Robert Duncanson and
sent to Robert Campbell of Glenlyon on
12 February 1692

GLENCOE'S GLOOM

We drove home to St Fillans through the gloomy valley of Glencoe, as dark and dreadful as if the massacre had just taken place.

BERTRAND RUSSELL, *Autobiography*
(1967-9; rept. London: Unwin Paperbacks
1978, p.561)

GLENCOE

Many places have evil reputations. Few, at first seeing, live up to those reputations. But there are a few. In Scotland, the Pass of Glencoe, the scene of the infamous massacre, is one of them.

ALISTAIR MacLEAN, *When Eight Bells Toll*
(1966; rept. London: Fontana Books 1967,
p.82)

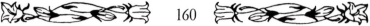

GREENOCK

> [T]his grey town
> That pipes the morning up before the lark
> With shrieking steam, and from a hundred stalks
> Lacquers the sooty sky; where hammers clang
> On iron hulls, and cranes in harbours creak,
> Rattle and swing, whole cargoes on their necks;
> Where men sweat gold that others hoard or spend,
> And lurk like vermin in their narrow streets:
> This old grey town, this firth, the further strand
> Spangled with hamlets, and the wooded steeps,
> Whose rocky tops behind each other press,
> Fantastically carved like antique helms
> High-hung in heaven's cloudy armoury,
> Is world enough for me.

JOHN DAVIDSON, 'A Ballad in Blank Verse
of the Making of a Poet' (*Ballads and Songs*,
1894)

HEBRIDES

> From the lone shieling of the misty island
>   Mountains divide us, and the waste of seas –
> Yet still the blood is strong, the heart is Highland,
>   And we in dreams behold the Hebrides.

ANONYMOUS, 'Canadian Boat Song'
in *Blackwood's Magazine* September 1829

IRVINE AND THE PRESS-GANG

The town was awakened with the din, as with the cry of fire; and lights came starting forward, as it were, to the windows. The women were out with lamentations and vows of vengeance. I was in a state of horror unspeakable. Then came some three or four of the press-gang, with a struggling sailor in their clutches, with nothing but his trowsers on, his shirt riven from his back in the fury. Syne came the rest of the gang,

and their officers, scattered, as it were, with a tempest of mud and stones, pursued and battered by a troop of desperate women and weans, whose fathers and brothers were in jeopardy. And these were followed by the wailing wife of the pressed man, with her five bairns, clamouring in their agony to Heaven against the king and government for the outrage.

JOHN GALT, *The Provost* (1822, Ch. 21)

KINNAIRD

I go North to cold, to home, to Kinnaird,
Fit monument for our time.

This is the outermost edge of Buchan.
Inland the sea birds range,
The tree's leaf has salt upon it,
The tree turns to the low stone wall.

GEORGE BRUCE, 'Kinnaird Head',
Collected Poems (Edinburgh: Edinburgh
University Press 1970, p.8)

KINTYRE

Without Kintyre Scotland wouldn't have a leg to stand on.

Kintyre saying.

LACHIN Y GAIR

Yet Caledonia, beloved are thy mountains,
    Round their white summits though elements war,
Though cataracts foam 'stead of smooth-flowing fountains,
    I sigh for the valley of dark Loch na Garr.

LORD BYRON (1788-1824), 'Lachin Y Gair'

LAMMERMUIR

They are sweeping over the Earnscleuch hill,

Where the silver mist hangs thin and still.
Their horses' hoofs from the heather flowers
Scatter the bloom in purple showers

LADY JOHN SCOTT (1810-1900),
'A Ride over Lammermuir'

LEWIS, THE BARE ISLAND

We crossed by ferry to the bare island
where sheep and cows stared coldly through the wind –
the sea behind us with its silver water,
the silent ferryman standing in the stern
clutching his coat about him like old iron.

IAIN CRICHTON SMITH, 'By Ferry to the
Island', *Selected Poems 1955-1980* (Edinburgh:
Macdonald 1981, p.22)

LEWIS

Tinkers subdued to council houses learn
to live as others do, earn as they earn
and English growing as the Gaelic dies
describes these vast and towering inland skies.
God is surrendering to other gods
as the stony moor to multiplying roads.
Folk songs and country westerns in the bars
displace the native music sweet and harsh
which dilettantes soon will learn to prize
when the last real brutal singer dies,
too zealous and too tearful. Ah, those eves
of fine September moons and autumn sheaves
when no-one knocked on doors, and fish was free,
before the Bible faded to TV
and tractors ground the bones of horses down
into bone-meal well suited to the town,
and girls were simple who drink brandies now

and wear mascara who would milk the cow.

IAIN CRICHTON SMITH, 'Deer on
the High Hills', *Selected Poems 1955-1980 (ibid,*
p.129)

MELROSE

If thou would'st view fair Melrose aright,
Go visit it by the pale moonlight;
For the gay beams of lightsome day
Gild, but to flout, the ruins grey.

SIR WALTER SCOTT,
The Lay of the Last Minstrel (1805, II.1.)

OCHILTREE

This old village Ochiltree . . . shows us better than any other
village we know of, the story of the emergence of Scotland
from the feudal to the philanthropic or modern age.

FRANCIS H. WALKER, *Morning Musings*
(Kilmarnock: The Standard Press 1929, p.6)

PEEBLES

Priorsford [= Peebles] . . . seemed . . . the very ideal of a
country town . . . Inns and houses that held some of the
graciousness of age were neighboured by shops and a cinema
built in a new and fantastic mode, but the prevailing
atmosphere was of the past, for, on the right-hand side of the
street, going towards the Mercat Cross, stood a fine old
building with turrets and narrow windows and steep-pitched
roof.

O. DOUGLAS, *The House That is Our Own*
(1940; rept. London: Hodder and Stoughton
1949, p.101)

RACKWICK

There is a fringe of tilth and pasture in the north of Hoy [in Orkney], along the shore: the road goes this far. Another road branches westward between the hills, into utter desolation, a place of kestrels and peatbogs. One thinks of the psalmist and his vale of death. After five miles the road ends abruptly at a glint of sea and the farm of Glen. The dark hills are still all round, but they hold in their scarred hands a green valley. This is Rackwick. The bowl is tilted seawards – its lip is a curving bay, half huge round sea-sculptured boulders, half sand. Out in the bay, like guardians, stand two huge cliffs, The Sneuk and The Too.

GEORGE MacKAY BROWN,
An Orkney Tapestry (1969; rept. London:
Quartet Books 1973, p.27)

ST ANDREWS

St Andrews by the northern sea,
A haunted town it is to me!
A little city, worn and gray,
    The gray North Ocean girds it round;
And o'er the rocks, and up the bay,
    The long sea-rollers surge and sound;
And still the thin and biting spray
    Drives down the melancholy street,
And still endure, and still decay,
    Towers that the salt winds vainly beat.
Ghost-like and shadowy they stand
Dim-mirrored in the wet sea-sand.

ANDREW LANG (1844-1912),
'Almae Matres'

ST ANDREWS, CITY OF GOLF

Would you like to see a city given over,
Soul and body, to a tyrannising game?

If you would, there's little need to be a rover,
For St Andrews is the abject city's name.

ROBERT F. MURRAY (1863-94),
'The City of Golf'

ST ANDREWS CATHEDRAL

And yonder, doun by the Pends whaur time hes duin
Havoc on the auld toun waas, is Scotland's Shame,
Hame nou for the daws, the doos and the craws,
The jauggy ruins o white wes in its time
Europe's grandest cathedral, no even York
Milan, nor Rheims, nor Köln surpassan it –
There oor culture, oor Renaissance fell
And we, Sant-Aundraes, aa oor fowk fell wi't!
Ither lands their peerless buildins vaunt
And Scotland her incomparable ruins.
O whit a wound is there for aa to see
Whaur stood aa Scotland's culture shrined in stane:
For wi it's gane oor leids, oor croon, oor state
Oor parliament, oor sauls, aa betrayed
For a puckle English gowd in a few pooches,
Oor sons enslaved ti' Babylon-on-Thames.

TOM SCOTT, *Brand the Builder*
(Epping: Ember Press 1975, p.4)

ST KILDA

The inhabitants of the island of St Kilda, to this day, are no
better than savages; they are few in number, and live upon
stinking fish, and rotten eggs, laid by birds in the hollows of
the rocks. They will touch neither eggs nor fish until they are
in a state of putrefaction. They are little known to the rest of
the world, and very seldom visited; and lucky for them that
this is the case, or the race of Kildaites would soon be extinct
by frequent hemorrhages; for it is confidently affirmed that the
instant a stranger touches the shore, the noses of all the

natives begin to bleed throughout the island.

SARAH MURRAY, *The Beauties of Scotland*
(1799; rept. Hawick: Byway Books 1982,
p.193)

ST MONANS

St Monans bore me.
A salt-splashed cradle with a golden fringe.
And even now, it is that same cradle that rocks me nightly
towards my grave.

CHRISTOPHER RUSH, *Peace Comes
Dropping Slow* (Edinburgh: Ramsay Head
Press 1983, p.1)

SKYE

Skye is often raining, but also fine: hardly embodied; semi-transparent; like living in a jelly fish lit up with green light.
Remote as Samoa; deserted: prehistoric. No room for more.

VIRGINIA WOOLF, postcard of 27 June
1938 to Duncan Grant (in ed. Nigel Nicolson,
The Letters of Virginia Woolf, vol. 6 London:
Chatto and Windus 1980, p.248)

SKYE, GREAT ISLAND

O great Island, Island of my love,
many a night of them I fancied
the great ocean itself restless
agitated with love of you
as you lay on the sea,
great beautiful bird of Scotland,
your supremely beautiful wings bent
about many-nooked Loch Bracadale,
your beautiful wings prostrate on the sea
from the Wild Stallion to the Aird of Sleat,

your joyous wings spread
about Loch Snizort and the world.

SORLEY MacLEAN, 'The Island' (translated
from his Gaelic original), *Spring tide and Neap
tide* (Edinburgh: Canongate 1977, pp.72-3)

SUILVEN

Suilven standing up in the west like a huge grape-dark hand, miles away above the desolate moorland. What were the mountains of Switzerland compared with that shape of stone solitary as a mammoth upon the edge of the landscape?

COMPTON MacKENZIE, *The East Wind of
Love* (1937: rept. London: Chatto and Windus
1973, p.263)

SUILVEN AND CUL MOR

I watch, across the loch
where seatrout are leaping,
Suilven and Cul Mor, my
mountains of mountains,
looming and pachydermatous in the thin light
of a clear half moon.

NORMAN MacCAIG, 'Above Inverkirkaig',
Old Maps and New (London: The Hogarth
Press 1978, p.85)

TROSSACHS

This solitude, the romance and wild loveliness of everything here [the Trossachs], the absence of hotels and beggars, the independent simple people, who all speak Gaelic here, all make beloved Scotland the proudest, finest country in the world. Then there is that beautiful heather, which you do not see elsewhere. I prefer it greatly to Switzerland, magnificent and glorious as the scenery of that country is.

QUEEN VICTORIA, Highland Journal,
2 September 1869

TWEEDSIDE

Just as Cicero said of Athens, that in every stone you tread on history, so on Tweedside by every nook and valley you find the place of a ballad, a story, or a legend.

ANDREW LANG, *Lost Leaders*
(London: Kegan Paul 1889, p.4)

YARROW

I dreamed a dreary dream this night,
 That fills my heart wi sorrow;
I dreamed I was pouing the heather green
 Upon the braes of Yarrow.

ANON, 'The Braes o Yarrow', in Francis James Child, *The English and Scottish Popular Ballads* (1882-98, 214A)

12

STATE OF THE SCOTTISH NATION

AFTER ALEXANDER

Sen Alexander our king wes deid
    That Scotland left in luve and lee,   *peacetime*
Away was sonse of aill and bred,   *abundance*
    Of wine and wax, of gamin and glee.   *entertainment*
The gold was changit all in leid,
    The frute failyeit on everilk tree.
Christ succour Scotland and remeid   *remedy*
    That stad is in perplexitie.   *in a condition of*

ANON, in Wyntoun's *Orygynale Cronykill of Scotland* (1795)

THE SELLING OF SCOTLAND

Our Duiks were deills, our Marquesses were mad,
Our Earls were evil, our Viscounts yet more bad,
Our Lords were villains, and our Barons knaves
    Who wish our burrows did sell us for slaves.

They sold the church, they sold the State and Nation,
They sold their honour, name and reputation,
They sold their birthright, peerages and places
    And now they leave the House with angrie faces.

ANON (1707), 'Verses on the Scots Peers, 1706'

A FORCED UNION

From a forced and divided Union
And from the church and kirk communion
Where Lordly prelates have dominion
    Deliver us, Lord.

171

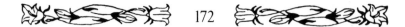

From a new transubstantiation
Of the old Scots into ane English nation
And from all the foes to Reformation
Deliver us, Lord.

ANON (1707), 'A Litanie Anent the Union'

FREEDOM

A! Freedom is a noble thing!
Freedom makis man to have liking,
Freedom all solace to man givis:
He livis at ease that freely livis!
A noble hart may have nane ease,
Na ellis nocht that may him please,
Gif freedom failye; for free liking
Is yarnit owre all othir thing.   *longed for*

JOHN BARBOUR (*c.* 1320-95), 'The Brus'

SURRENDER OF FREEDOM

I think I see a free and independent kingdom delivering up that which all the world hath been fighting for, since the days of Nimrod; yea, that for which most of all the Empires, Kingdoms, States and Principalities and Dukedoms of Europe, are at this time engaged in the most bloody and cruel wars that ever were, to wit a power to manage their own affairs by themselves without the assistance and counsel of any other.

LORD BELHAVEN, speech of 2 Nov 1706
against the parliamentary Union

MONSTROUS MONUMENT

Scotsmen, awake! You have nothing to lose but your English chains, glittering though they be with Britannia metal polish. If you do not soon arise from your Rip van Winkle sleep, and

achieve political independence, there is only one destiny awaiting you. You must order the tombstone of Scottish Freedom. Desecrate not the Field of Bannockburn with this abomination; but add the missing spray to the laurel-wreath of England by making Culloden the place of sepulture. When the English Premier has unveiled this monstrous monument to a people's self-betrayal, the assembled multitude of Anglicized mercenaries would read the appropriate epitaph: SACRED TO THE MEMORY OF THE REMAINS OF SCOTTISH CULTURE AND FREEDOM. 'For the glory of Scotland has departed'. (*Hosea* x.5.). R.I.P.

> WILLIAM BELL, *Rip Van Scotland*
> (London: Cecil Palmer 1930, pp.135-6)

ONLY FOR LIBERTY

For so long as one hundred men remain alive, we shall never under any conditions submit to the domination of the English. It is not for glory or riches or honours that we fight, but only for liberty, which no good man will consent to lose but with his life.

> BERNARD DE LINTON, *Declaration of Arbroath* (1320, translated by Lord Cooper of Culross)

LAND OF THE OMNIPOTENT NO

It is so
In Scotland, land of the omnipotent No.

> ALAN BOLD, 'A Memory of Death',
> *In This Corner: Selected Poems 1963-83*
> (Edinburgh: Macdonald 1983, p.40)

SCOTLAND THE WEE

Scotland the wee, crèche of the soul,
of thee I sing

land of the millionaire draper, whisky vomit
and the Hillman Imp

TOM BUCHAN, 'Scotland the Wee',
Dolphins at Cochin (London: Barrie and Rockliff
1969, p.34)

A SOUR SPIRIT

In no civilised country is toleration so little understood as in
Scotland . . . The result is that there runs through the entire
country a sour and fanatical spirit, an aversion to innocent
gaiety, a disposition to limit the enjoyment of others, and a
love of inquiring into the opinions of others, and of interfering
with them, such as is hardly anywhere else to be found.

HENRY THOMAS BUCKLE, *History of
Civilisation in England* (1861, Vol. III)

THE GLOOM OF THE MIDDLE AGES

Time rolled on; one generation succeeded another; the
eighteenth century passed away; the nineteenth century came,
and still the people made no sign [of enlightenment]. The
gloom of the middle ages was yet upon them. When all
around was light, the Scotch, enveloped in mist, crept on,
groping their way, dismally and with fear. While other nations
were shaking off their old superstitions the Scotch clung to
theirs with undiminished tenacity.

HENRY THOMAS BUCKLE, *History of
Civilisation in England* (1861, Vol. III)

SCOTS, WHA HAE

Scots, wha hae wi' Wallace bled,
Scots, wham Bruce has aften led,
Welcome to your gory bed
Or to victorie!

Now's the day, and now's the hour;
See the front o' battle lour,
See approach proud Edward's power –
    Chains and Slaverie!

ROBERT BURNS (1759-96),
'Scots, Wha Hae'

A GLIMPSE OF AULD LANG SYNE

But I am half a Scot by birth, and bred
    A whole one, and my heart flies to my head

As Auld Lang Syne brings Scotland, one and all,
    Scotch plaids, Scotch snoods, the blue hills, and clear streams,
The Dee, the Don, Balgounie's Brig's black wall,
    All my boy feelings, all my gentler dreams
Of what I then dreamt, clothed in their own pall,
    Like Banquo's offspring. Floating past me seems
My childhood in this childishness of mine; .
    I care not – 'tis a glimpse of Auld Lang Syne.

LORD BYRON, *Don Juan* (1819-24, X, 17-18)

A PERPETUALLY DEPRESSED AREA

Over the centuries the Scots have accepted the fact of English domination. You've only got to look at the figures to realise Scotland is a perpetually depressed area. Why else do the Scots have to leave Scotland to make a good living?

SEAN CONNERY, in Kenneth Passingham,
Sean Connery (London: Sidgwick and Jackson
1983, p.98)

THE CURSE OF UNION

Black be the day that e'er to England's ground
Scotland was eikit by the UNION's bond . . .   *joined*

ROBERT FERGUSSON (1750-74)
'The Ghaists; A Kirk-yard Eclogue'

THE LAND

Scotland lived, she could never die, the land would outlast them all, their wars and their Argentines, and the winds come sailing over the Grampians still with their storms and rain and the dew that ripened the crops – long and long after all their little vexings in the evening light were dead and done.

> LEWIS GRASSIC GIBBON, *Sunset Song*
> (1932; rept. in *A Scots Quair*, London:
> Pan Books 1982, p.213)

TRAITORS

I regret, as a Scotsman, because we have always had a good name for business, that those Judases who sold our country [in 1707], got so little for themselves. £26,000! Why, their patron saint, Judas, got almost as much, taking into consideration the greater purchasing power of money when he did his deal.

> R.B. CUNNINGHAME GRAHAM,
> speech of 18 June 1927 at Stirling

THE ENEMY WITHIN

The enemies of Scottish nationalism are not the English, for they were ever a great and generous folk, quick to respond when justice calls. Our real enemies are among us, born without imagination.

> R.B. CUNNINGHAME GRAHAM,
> speech of 21 June 1930

BENEATH THE SURFACE

The truth is that we are a nation of arselickers, though we disguise it with surfaces: a surface of generous, openhanded manliness, a surface of dour practical integrity, a surface of futile maudlin defiance like when we break goalposts and windows after football matches on foreign soil and commit suicide on Hogmanay by leaping from fountains in Trafalgar Square.

ALASDAIR GRAY, *1982 Janine*
(London: Jonathan Cape 1984, pp.65-6)

WIRED FOR WAR

Scotland is wired for war, especially the bit north-west of Glasgow. The Nato nuclear bombers have come to the Isle of Skye. Apart from a handful of landowners and clergymen the local folk do not want them, but no government need be moved by the wishes of the northern native, especially not the Gaelic native. Down waterlanes on the Firth of Clyde American and British missile submarines slip to and from their fuel bases. Between Loch Lomond and Gareloch one hill at least is honeycombed with galleries where the multi-megaton warheads are stockpiled.

ALASDAIR GRAY, *1982 Janine*
(*ibid*, p.134)

SCOTLAND'S RESOURCES

I realised that Scotland was shaped like a fat messy woman with a surprisingly slender waist. A threestranded belt of road, canal and railway crossed that waist joining Edinburgh, and the ports facing Europe to Glasgow and the ports facing Ireland and America. And the woman was rich! She had enough land to feed us all if we used her properly, and sealochs and pure rivers for fish-farming, and hills to grow timber on. Her native iron was exhausted, but we had coalbeds which would last another two centuries, and a skilled industrial population who could make anything in the heavy-engineering line.

ALASDAIR GRAY, *1982 Janine*
(*ibid*, p.281)

THE LAND THAT BEGAT ME

This is my country,
The land that begat me,
These windy spaces
Are surely my own.
And those who here toil
In the sweat of their faces
Are flesh of my flesh,
And bone of my bone.

ALEXANDER GRAY (1882-1968), 'Scotland'

THE SCOTTISH LORDS

The Scottish dukes are traditionally loathed by their people,
especially Argyll, Sutherland, Montrose, Hamilton and
Buccleuch. The immorality, cruelty and avarice of their
forebears have scarred Scots' souls forever. Their descendants
still hold sway, owning thousands of acres and clinging to a
feudal landed power that was won by men with the morals of
tomcats.

WILLIE HAMILTON, *My Queen and I*
(London: Quartet Books 1975, p.131)

A ROCH WIND

Roch the wind in the clear day's daw-in',   *rough*
  Blaws the cloods heelster gowdy ow'r the bay.
But there's mair nor a roch wind blawin'
  Through the great glen o' the warld the day.
It's a thocht that will gar oot rottans –
  A' they rogues that gang gallus fresh and gay –
Tak' the road an' seek ither loanins
  For their ill ploys tae sport an' play.

HAMISH HENDERSON (born 1919),
'The Freedom Come All Ye'

ABUNDANCE

When that I had oversene this Regioun,
The whilk, of nature, is both gude and fair,
I did propose ane litill questioun,   *propose*
Beseikand her the same for to declare:
What is the cause our boundis bene so bare?
Quod I: or what dois muve our Miserie?
Or whereof dois proceid our povertie?

For, throu the support of your hie prudence,
Of Scotland I persave the properties,
And, als, consideris, by experience,
Of this countrie the great commodities.
First, the aboundance of fishis in our seas,
And fructual mountanis for our bestiale;
And, for our cornis, mony lusty vale;

The rich Riveris, pleasand and profitabill;
The lustie lochis, with fish of sindry kindis;
Hunting, hawking, for nobillis convenabill;
Forrestis full of Dae, Rae, Hartis, and Hyndis;
The fresh fountainis, whose holesum cristal strandis
Refreshis so the fair fluriste green meadis:
So laik we no thing that to nature needis.

SIR DAVID LINDSAY (*c.* 1490-1555),
'The Dreme'

JOHN THE COMMON-WEAL
ON CORRUPTION

I pray you, sir, begin first at the Border,
For how can we feud us against England,
When we can not, without our native land,
Destroy our own Scots, common traitor thieves,
Who to loyal labourers daily do mischief?

SIR DAVID LINDSAY (*c.* 1490-1555), in
Robert Kemp's acting version of *The Satire of
the Three Estates* (London: Heinemann 1951,
p.49)

GOOD COUNSEL ON THE COMMON-WEAL

Because the Common-Weal has been o'er lookèd,
That is the cause that Common-Weal is crookèd.
With singular profit he has been so suppressed,
That he is both cold, naked and disguised.

SIR DAVID LINDSAY (*c.* 1490-1555), in
Robert Kemp's acting version of *The Satire of
the Three Estates* (*ibid*, p.58)

THE ALBANNAICH

The Albannaich, whoever they were, the collection of actual human persons assembled in the distant past in the geographical area we call Scotland, turned out to have been initially gifted with the element of sheer talent to a degree that had no parallel elsewhere.

FIONN MacCOLLA, *At the Sign of the Clenched
Fist* (Edinburgh: Macdonald 1967, p.202)

THE BARREN FIG

*O Scotland is
THE barren fig.
Up, carles, up*   *men*
And roon it jig.

*Auld Moses took
A dry stick and
Instantly it
Floo'ered in his hand.*

*Pu' Scotland up,
And wha can say
It winna bud
And blossom tae.*

A miracle's
Oor only chance.
Up, carles, up
And let us dance!

> HUGH MacDIARMID, 'A Drunk Man Looks
> at the Thistle', *Complete Poems 1920-1976,*
> eds. W.R. Aitken and Michael Grieve
> (London: Martin Brian and O'Keeffe 1978,
> pp.105-6)

THE THISTLE RISES

The thistle rises and forever will,
Getherin' the generations under't.
This is the monument o' a' they were,
And a' they hoped and wondered.

> HUGH MacDIARMID, 'A Drunk Man Looks
> at the Thistle', (*ibid*, p.152)

SCOTLAND AND ETERNITY

Whatever Scotland is to me,
Be it aye part o' a' men see
O' Earth and o' Eternity

> HUGH MacDIARMID, 'A Drunk Man Looks
> at the Thistle', *Complete Poems 1920-1976,*
> (*ibid*, p.161)

THE STATE THAT SCOTLAND'S IN

Lourd on my hert as winter lies
The state that Scotland's in the day.
Spring to the North has aye come slow
But noo dour winter's like to stay
*   For guid,*
*   And no' for guid!*

> HUGH MacDIARMID, 'To Circumjack
> Cencrastus', *Complete Poems 1920-1976,*
> (*ibid*, p.204)

THE LITTLE WHITE ROSE

The rose of all the world is not for me.
I want for my part
Only the little white rose of Scotland
That smells sharp and sweet – and breaks the heart.

HUGH MacDIARMID, 'The Little White
Rose', *Complete Poems 1920-76*, (*ibid*, p.461)

SCOTLAND SMALL?

Scotland small? Our multiform, our infinite Scotland *small?*
Only as a patch of hillside may be a cliché corner
To a fool who cries 'Nothing but heather!' . . .

HUGH MacDIARMID, 'Direadh 1',
Complete Poems 1920-1976, (*ibid*, p.1170)

THE COMMUNISM OF THE CLANS

Scotland must again have Independence, but not to be ruled
by traitor kings and chiefs, lawyers and politicians. The
Communism of the clans must be re-established on a modern
basis . . . The country must have one clan, as it were – a united
people working in co-operation and co-operatively using the
wealth that is created.

JOHN MacLEAN, 'All Hail! The Scottish
Communist Republic' (pamphlet of 1920)

NATIONALITY

Of course one doesn't deliberately set about being a Scot . . . If
one is content to be oneself, one's nationality will make itself
felt unobtrusively, like the scent of a flower.

F. MARIAN McNEILL, *The Scots Cellar*
(1956; rept. London: Granada 1981, p.124)

PERPETUAL CHILDHOOD

A grippy nation like oors canna but learn   *griping*
    tae pit its mou tae the bottle.   *mouth*
Or, gin it's teem, sook its ain thoomb.   *empty*

> KEN MORRICE, 'Cavl Kail', *For All I Know*
> (Aberdeen University Press 1981, p.16)

THE CAUSE OF THE PEOPLE

Gentlemen, from my infancy to this moment I have devoted myself to the cause of the people. It is a good cause – it shall ultimately prevail – it shall finally triumph.

> THOMAS MUIR, speech at his trial,
> 30 August 1793

SCOTCHED

Scotch God
Kent His
Faither.

Scotch Religion
Damn
Aa.

Scotch Equality
Kaa the feet frae
Thon big bastard.

Scotch Optimism
Through a gless,
Darkly.

Scotch Pessimism
Nae
Gless.

Scotch Sex
In atween
Drinks.

ALEXANDER SCOTT (born 1920),
'Scotched'

MY NATIVE LAND

Breathes there the man, with soul so dead,
Who never to himself hath said,
    This is my own, my native land!
Whose heart hath ne'er within him burn'd,
As home his footsteps he hath turn'd,
    From wandering on a foreign strand!

SIR WALTER SCOTT,
The Lay of the Last Minstrel (1805, 6.1)

LAND OF THE MOUNTAIN AND THE FLOOD

O Caledonia! stern and wild,
Meet nurse for a poetic child!
Land of brown heath and shaggy wood,
Land of the mountain and the flood,
Land of my sires! what mortal hand
Can e'er untie the filial band,
That knits me to thy rugged strand!

(Ibid, 6.11)

DESTRUCTION OF NATIONALITY

They are gradually destroying what remains of nationality, and making the country *tabula rasa* for doctrines of bold innovation. Their loosening and grinding down all those peculiarities which distinguished us as Scotsmen will throw the country into a state in which it will be universally turned to democracy, and instead of canny Saunders, they will have a

very dangerous North British neighbourhood.

SIR WALTER SCOTT, *Journal* 14 March
1826.

DIVERSITY

But till Ben-Nevis be level with Norfolkshire, though the
natural wants of the two nations [Scotland and England] may
be the same, the extent of these wants, natural or commercial,
and the mode of supplying them, must be widely different, let
the rule of uniformity be as absolute as it will.

SIR WALTER SCOTT, *Letters of Malachi
Malagrowther* (1826, First Letter)

SCOTTISH IDENTITY

For God's sake, sir, let us remain as Nature made us,
Englishmen, Irishmen, and Scotchmen, with something like
the impress of our several countries upon each!

SIR WALTER SCOTT, *Letters of Malachi
Malagrowther* (1826, Letter Second)

DELIVERANCE

By the union with England, the middling and inferior ranks of
people in Scotland gained a compleat deliverance from the
power of an aristocracy which had always before oppressed
them.

ADAM SMITH, *The Wealth of Nations*
(1784 edtn, Bk. V, Ch. iii)

BEHIND CASTLE WALLS

Scotland is like a bonnie woman pent
Ahint castle waas. The castle maun be   *walls*
Forced and she deiiverit frae her bands

SYDNEY GOODSIR SMITH, *The Wallace*
(Edinburgh: Oliver and Boyd 1960, p.122)

SCOTLAND AND ENGLAND

I do not think I could enjoy Life with greater Relish in any part of the world than in Scotland among you and your Friends, and I often amuse my Imagination with schemes for attaining that Degree of Happiness, which, however, is altogether out of my Reach. I am heartily tired of this Land of Indifference [England] and Phlegm where the finer Sensations of the Soul are not felt, and Felicity is held to consist in stupifying Port and overgrown Buttocks of Beef, where Genius is lost, Learning undervalued, and Taste altogether extinguished, and Ignorance prevails to such a degree that one of our Chelsea Club asked me if the weather was good when I crossed the Sea from Scotland . . .

TOBIAS SMOLLETT, letter of 1 March 1754
to Alexander Carlyle, in ed. L.M. Knapp,
The Letters of Tobias Smollett (Oxford:
Clarendon Press 1970, p.33)

A SENSE OF IDENTITY

For that is the mark of the Scot of all classes: that he stands in an attitude towards the past unthinkable to Englishmen, and remembers and cherishes the memory of his forebears, good or bad; and there burns alive in him a sense of identity with the dead even to the twentieth generation.

ROBERT LOUIS STEVENSON,
Weir of Hermiston (1896, Ch. 5)

A SMALLTIME DUMP

We knew our country was a smalltime dump
where nothing ever happened and
there was nothing to do.
And nobody had a name like Jelly Roll Morton.

GORDON WILLIAMS, *Walk Don't Walk*
(1972; rept. London: Alison and Busby 1980,
p.2)

THIS ANCIENT KINGDOM

I have a great many melancholy thoughts of living to see this ancient kingdom made a province, and not only our religious and civil liberties lost, but lost irrevocably, and this is the most dismal aspect ane incorporating union has to me, that it puts matters past help.

ROBERT WODROW, letter of 30 May 1706
to George Serle

INDEX OF AUTHORS

189

SUBJECT INDEX OF FIRST LINES

The first lines of verse quotations are in *italic*; the opening phrases of prose quotations are in roman.

1 AS OTHERS SEE US

2 BATTLES ANCIENT AND MODERN

3 CHARACTERS REAL AND IMAGINARY

8 LANGUAGE

9 LOVE AND LUST

10 NATIONAL INSTITUTIONS

12 STATE OF THE SCOTTISH NATION